#Afterhours

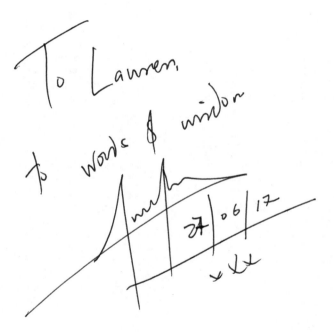

To Lauren,

to words & wisdom

27/06/12
x xx

#Afterhours

ANTHOLOGY / DIARY / MEMOIR / POEMS

Inua Ellams

and Selected Poets

Nine
Arches
Press

#Afterhours
Anthology / Diary / Memoir / Poems

Inua Ellams and Selected Poets

ISBN: 978-1-911027-16-4

First published April 2017 by:

Nine Arches Press
PO Box 6269
Rugby
CV21 9NL
United Kingdom

www.ninearchespress.com

Nine Arches Press is supported using public funding by the National Lottery through Arts Council England.

Supported using public funding by
**ARTS COUNCIL
ENGLAND**

We are grateful for the support of The National Poetry Library for helping to make this project and book possible.

To find out more about The National Poetry Library, please visit: **www.poetrylibrary.org.uk**

THE NATIONAL POETRY LIBRARY

SOUTHBANK CENTRE

Contents

#AFTERWORDS
by Chris McCabe

It is easy to relive the moment of the conception of *#Afterhours* as it has been captured in time-lapse film. The library was creating a live writing experiment called Global Love Poem in which visiting poets to the Southbank Centre would add a line to a collaborative sonnet. I would then climb up a ladder and spray-paint the lines on the wall. The film catches me scaling up and down a ladder, in shorts, spray-painting words, painting over typos, spraying again. The thing with time-lapse is that it already has us hurtling into the future as the footage races through already lived days, thousands of times quicker than they happened.

A minute into the film and Inua and I are standing at the fringe of the camera's lens. Inua is deciding upon what will be the the twelfth line for the sonnet. Michael Augustin, a German poet, had written the eleventh line which might well have left many poets at a loss to follow: "ah, love, that carnivorous flower snapping at me." Inua enjoyed the challenge and, in a move that surprised me, decided to extend the metaphor of the carnivorous flower. This line that could easily have proved a straitjacket was extended by Inua, and turned on itself, in a way that seems natural: "ah, love, that carnivorous flower snapping at me / is a hundred pitchers of honey."

Here was a poet extremely at ease with the idea of engaging in dialogue with other poets, who sensed intuitively that poetry is born from the sparks that fly from the hinges between poems, that believed in the community that bonds poets from around the world together. This would be significant for what we talked about next, though time-lapse blurs memory. I recall standing in front of the nearly-completed exhibition poem for an hour, spray paint dissolving in dry air, as Inua described the project which would become *#Afterhours*.

The project would need a larger canvas than the one on the wall behind us, and more poets than the twelve it took to complete the Global Love Poem. What Inua was describing wouldn't take a weekend of the Poetry International Festival at Southbank Centre to complete: it would require twelve months of dedicated writing and the whole of the library's collection.

Projects don't end and begin, they're linked at the arm like paper-chain people. As Inua leaves the time-lapse and I push the ladder aside, the poem on the wall now within easy reach from the floor, I was already looking ahead to the project which would become #*Afterhours.* I pictured Inua heading off with a miner's light to plunder the depths of the collection and, if I strained, I could hear the canary song that he would bring back for us.

When the project began three months later, and Inua arrived for the first of his many days at the library, I began to wonder if his role was as a poet-in-residence or – that more dedicated thing – a reader-in-residence? What excited me from the off was this vocalisation and demonstration of how all poets must begin as readers and – to become the poets they know they can be – continue to read as part of their practice. An alternative title for this project could be #*Afterwords:* as far as the language arts go, there's no meaningful new work that doesn't relate back to the breakthroughs of previous generations. As the child is father to the man, the reader is always parent to the poet: poets are nurtured and sustained by this bond. As well show the muse the Fire Exit than give up on reading. Many poets have tried to hide their relationship with what they read, to suggest that their individual gift arrives to them like stigmata, a branded blessing from their DNA. But it's never true. At least not for any poet worth reading – and there, in that word 'reading', is the loop back to the source of all creativity in language. It begins, it began, with the pleasure of text from a page spilling over into another's imagination.

What #*Afterhours* shows us is that there is a right way to respond to poems that have existed in the world before the new ones about to be written. You do it through passion and a love of the art, a desire to share the joy you have found in what you have read. You do it through open response and dialogue with the poet who came before you and you do it through making the poem you are writing your own. You do it through respectful credit and acknowledgement of the poet who triggered the switch, even after the ejector seat of your own poem finds its own Andromeda. Inua has done all of this. #*Afterhours* will be a guide to other poets and readers, navigating their way through the art.

Libraries are centres of creativity and the blog posts that Inua wrote for the library, and are published in this book, document this. Poetry responds to poetry, Yes, but it also thrives on lived experience. Inua wasn't a miner for books alone, he was a light-bearer back to the readers in the library. He talked to people. #*Afterhours* is one of those few, rare books, that lifts its own lid to show the teeming ecosystem of thought, dialogue and language-making that would otherwise be lost to us.

#*Afterhours* is a gift from a poet inviting us into their creative world, guiding us through the riches of The National Poetry Library. It is a gift from one reader to another.

Chris McCabe
Poetry Librarian, The National Poetry Library

INTRODUCTION

In 2014 I turned 30 and wished to mark it with a project about the end of childhood. I spoke with Chris McCabe, Librarian at The National Poetry Library, and explained the idea: to reconstruct my youth by writing response-poems to the work of British and Irish poets. I would find poems published between 1984 and 2002, from when I was born to when I turned 18, and stay as close as possible to aspects of the originals – subject matter, structure, syntax, length etc – but I would reset the poems. For instance, a poem on climbing a hill in southern England to watch roaming sheep could be reset to climbing a hill in northern Nigeria to watch wild antelope. I hoped the project would show the ways poetry transcends time, borders, history, culture, race and empire, to illustrate cultural differences and similarities.

I chose #*Afterhours* as a title because it summoned three aspects of the project: 1/ In poetry, the tradition of subtitling a poem informed by another poet with the word 'After' and the author's name. 2/ Turning 30 and approaching the 'noonlight' of my years, frames my youth as 'early hours', and the subsequent years as *after* those hours. 3/ For writers, the stereotype of 'burning the midnight oil' – working late after the standard hours of work.

Chris liked the idea and for the 12 month period it took to complete, #*Afterhours* was resident at The National Poetry Library. Without their immense collection, this project would simply not exist. I needed to find poems that were specific to British and Irish life, but with specificities that could be paralleled in Nigerian life. As a playwright and storyteller, I needed poems that were narrative, or whose forms allowed for narration. I also needed the poem-titles to be easily transposable or require little modification, all this I hoped would make my responses as close to the original as possible. As the project unfolded, I kept and published a diary on The National Poetry Library's website. Edited versions of those entries are gathered here alongside the poems I found, and my responses.

If you followed the original project as it happened and read the diary entries, you might notice the first poem I responded to, 'Unrelated Incidents' from *Intimate Voices* by Tom Leonard, is not included here; unfortunately we were not able to secure permission to publish the poem. As it was absolutely vital and integral to the *#Afterhours* project that we were able to publish every original poem alongside my response to it in each instance, I returned to the library and instead selected a poem by Iain Crichton Smith, 'No Return', with which to replace it. It was challenging, it felt akin to resetting the beginnings or exposition of a sonata *after* its completion, and over a year's time had passed between 'Unrelated Incidents' and 'No Return', but the process of seeking, deconstructing and rebuilding again, reaffirmed another context in which this project sits.

Whenever a poem that I feel contains inarguable truth, precision or clarity finds me, whenever a poem reflects my aesthetics or poetics, whenever a poem speaks directly to me, of me, for me, and were I to write on its topic, I would echo its entirety, I keep the poem. I save it. As soon as I can, I teach the poem in workshops, schools, universities, colleges. I share how I read it, how it might be read, and invite the interpretations of my students into the space. With the poem, I create conversation and community. At some point, always, I begin to speculate on what would need to change to make the poem more *me*. If it were set within my Muslim-Christian-Nigerian-English-Irish-Immigrant-Golden-age-of-hip-hop-hood, what would differ? What would stay the same? This impulse, to further *localise* a loved poem, was (and still is) a thrilling thought-experiment second only to the pleasure of reading poetry. In *#Afterhours*, I set out to actualise the experiment.

The tradition of writing response-poems is as old as poetry. One could argue that all poems are response-poems. Sir Walter Raleigh responded to Marlowe's 'The Passionate Shepherd to His Love', Elizabeth Bishop to Felicia Dorothea Hemans' 'Casabianca', Daniel Hall to Pound's 'In a Station of the Metro', Billy Collins to Auden's 'Musée des Beaux Arts', Annie Finch to Andrew Marvell's 'To His Coy Mistress', Suzanne Frischkorn to Neruda's 'Fable of the Mermaid and the Drunks'... the list is inextinguishable.

The difference is how closely I wanted to write. I did not want to work with a line, a verse, a structure, or an opposing stance, but instead respond to as much of the original poem as possible whilst writing about my childhood. For this reason, I had no intentions whatsoever of publishing my poems without the originals alongside. I wanted to narratively, culturally, historically translate and transpose those poems, to show, in utter transparency, that I was not the sole creator of the work I produced. Whereas writers are regularly told to hide their sources, I wanted to centre them. I hoped to demonstrate how poetry is always in dialogue with the world and with other worlds.

For 1988, I responded to Jo Shapcott's 'Photograph: Sheepshearing' with 'Photograph: Ram Sacrificing'. Jo's poem, which describes and dissects the labour of shearing sheep, is for me tightly wound with the problems of the performance of masculinity. It brought to mind an incident from my childhood when I was a practising Muslim. My uncles and I had to slaughter a ram. We would later divide the meat among our neighbours and friends, but I remembered befriending and feeding the animal, my horror at the thought of it dying, yet refusing to let my emotions show as we stood beside the bound-up animal, knives glinting in the sunlight above its throat. The richest readings of my version is summoned when it is paired with its predecessor.

All I have written are in one sense odes to the originals, and in that, odes to the poets.

I would like to thank them for seeing what I was attempting, for welcoming the project, giving publishing consent, and their publishers for generously allowing us to reproduce their poems.

I would also like to thank the staff at The National Poetry Library, Jessica Atkinson, Mia Farlane, Pascal O'Loughlin and Chris McCabe for embedding me within the fabric of the library and supporting the project in every way conceivable. Finally, I'd like to thank R.A. Villanueva, who sat beside and discussed with me many of the poems as they unfolded.

Inua Ellams
January 2017

29/10/14 // Diary Entry #1

Today is the first day of the #*Afterhours* project and I am excited and nervous at the task ahead: to rewrite my childhood *through* British poetry, writing poems after/in-response to poems published between the years 1984 and 2002, from when I was born to when I turned 18.

I first started writing poetry properly in 2002 when I returned to London from Dublin. It was tough to find work and I was unqualified in anything. I had time on my hands and a library card. The librarians I met pointed me to books on black history in the western world and when I say I spent a year becoming politicised and angry, I mean for the first time I grasped the horrors of colonialism and institutional racism and its continuing legacy from the words of its victims. I also quickly realised that the history most of the books discussed and archived, that of the transatlantic slave trade, wasn't my history. I was born in Nigeria, I am not Black British (or American, for that matter), I am not Caribbean, I am an African, and what I was reading, though it is branched out of my ancestral history, wasn't mine. This broadened the rabbit hole of the deep identity crisis I fell into during those early days, much of which I still unpack and explore. However, two books taught me to channel that anger: Malcolm X's and Audre Lorde's autobiographies.

Today, when I enter the Poetry Library, there are books laid out for a visiting school group. Half of the table is taken up by Sylvia Plath and Allen Ginsberg and the other half, exclusively by Audre Lorde's poetry. For various reasons, including the fleeting and fragmentary nature of poetry itself and work as a poet, further heightened by my full-time freelance arts-based work, I look for and rely on signs: little clues from the universe, God, or the various powers that order our wakings and our sleep, that I am doing the right thing at the right time. I take these books by Audre Lorde as a sign, as if pointing the way back to the anger of childhood, that I may write, discover and shed light on those years.

29/10/14// Revisited 05/11/16// Diary Entry #2

Today I begin again searching for the first poem of the *#Afterhours* project, in which I rewrite my childhood through British poetry.

The first attempt at this, the books I browsed through were recommended by staff at the Poetry Library: *A Tract Against The Giants* by Bill Griffiths, *Mister Punch* by David Harsent and *Intimate Voices* by Tom Leonard. I wrote:

***

"Bill Griffiths' poetry is crazy. Born in 1948 and part of one of the world's earliest sound poetry groups, I find his poems audacious, dense, abstract and experimental. The book has hand-written, drawn and illustrated sections, and though I really respect the wildly playful, adventurous nature of the collection, it isn't to my taste in poetry.

"David Harsent's book is dark. It is about Mr Punch (of Punch and Judy) but tells about his origins; a manic anti-hero, a court fool, a trickster, a misogynist. I try to find parallels. One of Nigeria's longest running newspapers is called *The Punch*, and was in circulation in 1984. I used to watch Punch and Judy shows back then. Can I write about Nigeria as a puppet? As Mr Punch himself? And his misogyny manifesting in the violent umbilical-chord cutting around my birth? Maybe there are two poems here and I'm trying to do too much?

"The last book is by Tom Leonard and within the first few pages, I know I will find what I am looking for here. Some of the poems are partially written in phonetic Glaswegian vernacular, which to my eyes, looks similar to Pidgin English spoken in Nigeria – the nuanced, tonal, shorter, faster, bastardisation of the English language. Pidgin isn't really a written language. Where I have failed in trying to spell Pidgin words as they sound, Tom excels...."

***

The rest of the of the diary entry can be found on the Poetry Library website, and I highly recommend the book by Tom Leonard. This time around, I read through three Poetry Society Book choices by Blake Morrison, Iain Crichton Smith and Craig Raine. *Dark Glasses* by Blake, is a beautiful book and shows Blake's many interests, range of tone, subject matter and approaches to writing. I whittle choices down to three poems: 'Our Domestic Voices', 'A Child In Winter' and 'Sleep On it' – which is about exhausted parents in a restaurant thinking about the challenges of parenting. This poem would allow for me to write about my parents in the first year of my birth. 'A Child In Winter' also affords this but as the season does not exist in Nigeria, the title is problematic to reset.

Iain Crichton Smith's book, *The Exiles*, is an intense, searching, layered articulation on what it means to leave and return. He writes from his Gaelic/Scottish backgrounds of living in Ireland and Australia. The theme of migration will come to underline much of this project but it feels too early to invite it into the mix. The poem that I may be able to work with, is 'Power Cut', which describes a world suddenly plunged into darkness, which in 1984 Nigeria was (and remains) a daily occurrence.

Craig Raine's book, *Rich*, is the most instantly promising. Divided into three sections, Part One is called 'Rich', Part Two 'A Silver Plate' and Part Three 'Poor'. Written in fluid prose, Part Two does one of the things I am trying to do with this project. It sheds light on Craig's early life, from his birth to the end of his childhood, particularly illuminating his parents. Another strong theme is religion and spirituality, which dominated my early life. The poems that grab me are the first and last in the book: 'Rich' and 'The first lesson'. They might also allow me to write in the voices of my parents.

05/11/14// Revisited 05/11/16// Diary Entry #3

Two weeks before I was born, my parents had no idea I had a twin sister, or rather, that my twin sister had a twin brother; that two tiny hearts were beating within my mother. I've joked about this a lot, about being born and instantly chasing chaos, that my parents had to prepare for a whole other mouth to feed and life to nurture and raise. What the incident points to is how questionable birthing facilities were in northern Nigeria at the time. Linked to that, it points to infant mortality rates across the country. Back then, children died of malnutrition, asphyxia, severe infection and a host of other ailments. Some deaths were mysterious and unexplained. Some families were struck so often they felt cursed by a spirit, who would be born to them as a child. They would care for the baby, it would die and in doing so inflict pain and heartache, only to be reborn and the cycle begin anew. Perhaps they were indeed cursed, who is to know? These spirit-children with deep ties to the land-before-life, who always died before puberty, were called Abiku or Ogbanje children, in two of Nigeria's three main languages. Abiku is the Yoruba term, and Ogbanje is the Igbo; the Igbo term's literal translation is "children who come and go". No equivalent exists for spirit children in Hausa (the third language and my father's tongue) or Isoko (my mother's tongue). However, I wonder if my parents feared at all that my twin sister or I might have been spirit-children.

***

On closer reading of Craig Raine's book of poems, I felt I could not make the poems work as well as I hoped. Each seemed as if the poem I would produce would be too close or too far a departure from the original, so I returned to Iain's book, *The Exiles*. There, I rediscover 'No Return'. The poem warns the reader of the perils of revisiting a place, advising that much would have changed, the island will be unrecognisable and the visit ultimately disappointing. On second reading, I note the hint of exoticism in the description of the island, full of 'horned cows', 'moonlight of astonishing beauty', 'midnight waters', 'old story-telling people', 'acres of a lost music', 'mountains blue in the evening', 'witches wizards harlequins jesters'. All of this is in stark contrast to the end, where the island becomes 'bare, bleak and windy'. The end brings to mind the Welsh word 'hiraeth':

> *Hiraeth*
> (n.) a homesickness for a home to which
> you cannot return, a home which maybe
> never was; the nostalgia, the yearning,
> the grief for the lost places of your past.

I wondered if I could reset/rewrite/translate/transpose 'No Return' as a message from my parents to me or my twin sister, fearing us Abiku or Ogbanje children, urging us to stay, trying to placate our hiraeth of the spirit world by listing its parallels with 'real' Nigeria. I will try to use the last words of each of Iain's lines as the last words of mine, and elements of each verse: description, fixation, detail etc.

If the Abiku or Ogbanje child-phenomena sounds familiar, perhaps you've read *The Famished Road* by Ben Okri, an epic novel awarded the Booker Prize in 1991. It's protagonist is Azaro, a spirit child, and Ben's incredibly vivid, haunting melancholic, desperate descriptions of the spirit world and its inhabitants won fans the world over. Often described as magical realism, to many Nigerians, Ben simply wrote about ordinary life. I search through the internet and find essays on *The Famished Road*. I dig out my old dog-eared copy and skim-read, sparkling at Ben's brilliance. I note loose descriptions to inspire mine, and this line of Ben's which had crept out of his novel and into his poetry: "There is wonder here and there is surprise in everything that you cannot see." I will try to reference this in my poem.

Next week, the poem will begin.

1984
Iain Crichton Smith
From the book *The Exiles*

NO RETURN

No, really you can't go back to
that island any more. The people
are growing more and more unlike you
and the fairy stories
have gone down to the grave in peace.

The wells are dry now and the long grasses
parched by their mouths, and the horned cows
have gone away to another country
where someone else's imagination
is fed daily on milk.

There were, you remember, sunsets
against which the black crows were seen
and a moonlight of astonishing beauty
calmed at midnight by waters
which you're not able to hear.

The old story-telling people
have gone home to their last houses
under the acres of a lost music.
These have all been sold now
to suave strangers with soft voices.

It is a great pity that your cottage
preserved in January by clear ice
and in June surrounded by daisies
has been sold to the same strangers
and the bent witches evicted.

If you were to return now the roofs
would appear lower, the walls would have no echoes,
the wavelike motion would be lost,
the attics where you read all day
would be crammed with antiques.

No, you cannot return to an island
expecting that the dances will be unchanged,
that the currency won't have altered,
that the mountains blue in the evening
will always remain so.

You can't dip your mouth in the pure spring
ever again or ever again be haunted
by the 'eternal sound of the ocean'.
Even the boats which you once rowed
have set off elsewhere.

The witches wizards harlequins jesters
have packed up their furniture and guitars.
The witches have gone home on their broomsticks
and the conjurors with their small horses
and tiny carts have departed

leaving the island bare, bleak and windy,
itself alone in its barren corner
composed of real rocks and real flowers
indifferent to the rumours and the stories
stony, persistent.

NO RETURN 1984
#*After* Iain Crichton Smith

No, you really cannot go back to that other world, to
that island. We've been waiting months. Those spirit-
folk you left behind grow more and more unlike you,
cause pains in your chest. Think of them as fairy tales.
This will ease your breath. This will bring you peace.

The ceaseless seas are dry now and the long grasses
parched, the white trees are leafless, the horned cows
hung, the storm birds have gone to another country –
let this overrun your memories and dull imagination.
Let Earth tether you. Focus on your mother's milk.

What you can remember of the chlorochrous sunsets,
forests where the blue antelope kings were last seen,
the jade-green moonlight's astonishing ultra beauty,
the bickering mountains calmed by midnight waters,
that world that calls to you, you'll find mirrored here.

The griots, the wise ones, the old story-telling people,
the aunties and uncles have returned to their houses
and what fills their space, that ache you hear, is music.
That is Sunny Ade's voice. That is a talking drum now,
those are called harmonies: the joy of synced voices.

Sorry for that sudden silence, that is a power outage.
Sorry for how soup-thick the dark is. It's a small price
we pay for constant warmth. The sun sings us praises.
Our skin knows its light. Once it welcomed strangers
who colonised our lives. We fought, had them evicted.

If you flew a thousand feet above us to Earth's roofs,
you will trace narratives like these: lines and echoes,
multitudes, magnitudes of struggles, loved ones lost,
kinsmen crucified, cultures crushed in the light of day.
These stories decorate your bloodline like antiques.

No, you can't return to those others shores. That land
won't recognise your tongue. Its dance has changed.
Your throat knows soil now, your tones have altered.
Your soft palate's battered from our tickling evenings
and spirit folk don't get jokes, will always remain so.

We have dipped you in the warmest Yankari's spring.
You've heard the call to prayer, you'll ever be haunted.
You've sipped of guava fruit, you've dribbled an ocean.
Think of the distance crossed, all those rivers rowed,
the drifts of mists you parted searching for elsewhere.

We feel them watching you: the contortionists, jesters,
masquerades, egunguns, other sprit brethren, guitar-
mouthed spectres, teeth of silver strings, broomsticks
for eyes, glowing coal for noses, hooves of wild horses.
We will stand night-watch until they have all departed.

Our world is complex: bare, fruitiful, still as it is windy.
There are unseen wonders in our most barren corners,
from clenched fists of rocks to open palms of flowers.
Take. With them make here home, weave new stories,
remake our myth; stay with us. We will be persistent.

19/11/14// Diary Entry #4

Today the task is to find 1985's poem. It is eerily quiet in the Poetry Library. Libraries are meant to be, but it is SO quiet the man beside me, as he stands to leave, apologises for the noise his pages made as they turned.

The Poetry Library staff have selected for me poems by Carol Ann Duffy, Basil Bunting, Paul Durcan, and Tony Harrison. I was not conscious that I was alive in 1985 and have no memories of the time so the poem I will write, like the previous poem, must come from a third person point of view or be in the voice of an older friend or member of my family. I've been itching to write in my mother's voice and hope that something in Duffy's book *Standing Female Nude* will provide space to explore that. With that lurking in the back of my mind, I begin with Basil.

Basil Bunting is incredible. Friend and editor Tom Chivers has talked to me about him for years but I never made the effort to read. Now I see the reason for Tom's persistence. About halfway through the Basil's *Briggflatts* (Bloodaxe Books), he writes:

> A mason times his mallet
> to a lark's twitter
> listening while the marble rests
> lays his rule
> at a letter's edge

Tight, compact, internal-half-rhyme, assonance galore. On the back cover of this *Collected Poems*, Basil writes "I have set down words as a musician pricks his score, not to be read in silence but to trace in the air a pattern of sound that may sometimes, I hope, be pleasing..." and it is just that to me, and constantly pleasing. However, Basil's voice doesn't allow for the fluid conversational tone I look to write in. I feel not only will I stray too far if I try to write anything in response, but because of

Basil's somewhat classical tone, whatever I write will be too forced and thoroughly un-Nigerian. I'm in search of middle grounds. I set him down and flick through Tony Harrison's *V*.

V (Bloodaxe Books) is a single epic poem, written in response to the desecration of graveyards in Leeds. The poem includes some of the desecrations and a back and forth between the poet and the vandal. Tony's poem caused a storm when it came out. Printed on the back cover are quotes from the *Daily Mail* newspaper which described it as "A torrent of four-letter filth" of "the most explicitly sexual language". Mary Whitehouse described it as a "Work of singular nastiness" and this edition contains some of the articles written about it at the time. The poem is indeed full of four-letter words, but I don't read them as shocking or overused. They are used, more often than not, in context, or in the voice of the vandal. Perhaps twenty-nine years ago, England was so conservative a place that the outrage was justified. A lot has changed, writing has changed and undoubtedly, this contributes to my indifference. In my work, however, I believe there are far more interesting ways to be offensive and shocking – should that be my goal – so I don't use such words. All this however detracts from the fragility of these poems and what they try to negotiate. Written in strict a,b,a,b c,d,c,d rhyme scheme, Tony writes:

> This pen's all I have of magic wand.
> I know this world's so torn but want no other
> except for dad who'd hoped from 'the beyond'
> a better life than this one, *with* mother.

In this next verse, he reminds me a lot of Luke Wright's work, scathing in its critique of Britain's class system which is often embodied in the arts. Of opera, he says; "in a world where you say nothing changes / it seemed a sort of prick-tease of the soul."

As much as I enjoy the book and find resonance on many levels, it is just too long to attempt to re-write for 1985. I need much shorter poems. Next week, I'll pore through the other poets.

26/11/14// Diary Entry #5

Today I am poring through Paul Durcan's *Life is A Dream* and Carol Ann Duffy's *Standing Female Nude*. *Standing Female Nude* came out in 1985 when I was a year old. Before I knew I was alive, Carol Ann was publishing books. There's something I find oddly inspiring and humbling in that. I think she has forgotten more poems than I have written. The same goes for Paul Durcan, but choosing a poem from Carol Ann's book widens the possibility of writing in my mother's voice, which is what I want to do. This is not to say, obviously, that I cannot reset a poem written by a man in my mother's voice, but there are topics male poets hardly write about, subjects they do not touch at all, which I know Carol Ann has, which will resonate stronger with my mother's concerns at the time. But first, Paul.

Paul Durcan is outrageous. The titles of his poems suggest their tone: 'The Man with five penises', 'Around the corner from Francis Bacon' and 'On falling in love with a salesman in a shoe shop'. In these poems he writes about a haulier's wife cheating on her husband, lusting after a bishop, having sex in a carwash as nuns peer through the car's window, and more. Paul is an Irishman and the stereotype of the Irish – always being up for the craic – is a box he ticks firmly over and again as he navigates themes of religion and family in these fluid, rich poems.

Carol Ann Duffy (coincidently!) is quoted on Paul's front cover saying "To have heard him read adds another pleasure to the reading of his work – but the voice speaks clearly on the page in poems of harrowing intimacy, politics and love" and notes on the inside sleeve begins "Famous for his electrifying poetry readings..." I lived in Ireland for three years and discovered, like in Nigeria, a rich oral tradition which lives in Paul's work and I make a mental note to try to see him live.

Of his 1985 poems, my favourite is '10.30 a.m. Mass, 16 June 1985' which reads like a short story. He describes a priest entering an altar like "a film star at an international airport". The priest tells about his father's passing, the father who gave up alcohol in his honour. To honour all fathers, the priest asks those in the congregation to stand, which they do reluctantly in stunned silence before a slow clap builds "Until the entire church was ablaze with clapping hands" until the writer began crying, wishing to tell of his father. Enjoyable as it is, it deals with masculinity, and I want to write about the first woman in my life.

There are other poems written in the voices of female characters but their lives differ too much my mother's. I enjoy 'The Jewish Bride', 'The Marriage Contract' and 'At The Funeral Of The Marriage'. As the final two are about the end of marriages and my parents are still together, to rewrite any of these would mean pushing beyond their essential subject matter, which is beyond the bounds of this project, so, I turn finally to Carol Ann's poems in *Standing Female Nude* (Picador).

* * *

Carol Ann's book must have been ground-breaking when it came out; confident, nuanced, lithe, yet sledge-hammer-like in its ability to emotionally knock you down and pull you into her many worlds. The first poem itself 'Girl Talking', written from the point of view of a Pakistani girl, hints at an illicit sexual relationship with a miller in a town in Pakistan. It brings to mind the dangerously powerful work of Warsan Shire, but Carol Ann is far more restrained. 'Lizzie, Six' is about sexual abuse and in 1985, when the Paedophile Information Exchange was a powerful political group, it must have been an incredible thing to publish:

Where are you going?
To play in the fields.
I'll give you fields,
bend over that chair.

'You Jane' reads almost as if written in response to Paul Durcan's poems. The title suggests a Tarzan of a man and the poem paints a harsh picture of married life. The first lines read "At night I fart a Guinness smell against the wife / who snuggles up to me after I've given her one" and the voices and vistas into British life just keep coming. The task is to find a poem with a narrative loose enough to hold my mother's experiences. By the end of the collection, I have settled on three: 'Terza Rima SW19' (suggested by the poet Claire Trévien), 'Free Will' and 'Letters From Deadmen'.

I will need to interview my mother about her life at the time and use her answers to populate the poems, but speaking briefly, 'Terza Rima' is about a couple out on date where the romance is interrupted by a kestrel hunting and killing its prey. In 'Free Will', a woman makes the difficult choice to give up her unborn child, a choice she regrets, and in 'Letters From Deadmen', dead men write back to the living.

I could replace the kestrel with an aeroplane – my father was travelling a lot around the time I was born and I imagine my mother questioned the longevity of her marriage. Perhaps the plane could be a symbol of doom as the kestrel is? I could replace the unborn child with my mother's career and the many things she gave up to raise us children in her early years; how her free will was shaken by having us.

I could write letters *TO* dead men instead? where my mother warns the spirits of dead Nigerian men off her new son, saying things will change hence forth, critiquing their legacy and subsequently the state of Nigeria at the time... I have questions to ask.

1985
Carol Ann Duffy
From the book *Standing Female Nude*

LETTERS FROM DEADMEN

Beneath the earth a perfect femur glows. I recall
a little pain and then a century of dust. Observe my anniversary,
place purple violets tenderly before the urn. You must.
No one can hear the mulching of the heart, which thrummed
with blood or drummed with love. Perhaps, by now,
your sadness will be less. Unless you still remember me.

I flung silver pigeons to grey air with secret messages
for men I had not met. Do they ever mention me
at work and was there weeping in the crematorium?
Dear wife, dear child, I hope you leave my room
exactly as it was. The pipe, the wireless and, of course,
the cricket photographs. They say we rest in peace.

Ash or loam. Scattered or slowly nagged by worms. I lie
above my parents in the family plot and I fit neatly
in a metal cask in ever-loving memory of myself.
They parted his garments, casting lots upon them
what every man should take. A crate of stout.
Small talk above the salmon sandwiches. Insurance men.

But here you cannot think. The voice-box imitates
the skeletons of leaves. Words snail imperceptibly and soundless
in the soil. Dear love, remember me. Give me biography
beyond these simple dates. Were there psalms and hired limousines?
All this eternally before my final breath and may
this find you as it leaves me here. Eventually.

LETTERS TO DEADMEN 1985
#*After* Carol Ann Duffy

Beneath the soil's shredded skin, six feet, perhaps
a little deeper, you are observing his anniversary.
Place of darkness, I feel your fingers reaching out.
No one, only I can hear your remnants mulching
with jealousy, straining for my son's young flesh.
Your time is done. Tonight, you will remember me.

I know you grandfather; I've heard the legend told
for the sake, how you brought Christ to our village,
at the elder's meeting, stabbed their ancient hearts.
Dear husband's grandfather, you too are guilty of
exactly the same chaos: split your own village down
the centre to Muslim and infidel, the fields aflame.

Ash rains generations on and your legacies hang
above us still. Grandfathers, you are haunting us.
In mother's flinch at my new name, you are there.
They echo you grandfather-in-law; your offspring,
whatever the topic, speak to me in anger, tongues:
small fists, teeth of stones, I am a scorned woman

but it will end now. Could you have known I'd sever
the chord? That where your legends meet, flowing
in my womb, I'd make a pit, juice of purging water?
Beyond your clutches, I've washed your grandson of
all your violence. Tonight he sleeps one year older.
This cloth holds my last drop, I press over his head.

17/12/14// Diary Entry #6

Last week, something quite lovely happened to me here at the Library. I'd just sat down to read through Michael Hofmann's *Acrimony* (where I will take a poem to rewrite for 1986) when I heard a throat clear, and a woman enquire if I was Inua Ellams. I responded affirmatively and she said she'd just spent the last few days re-reading my previous pamphlets of poems, and on her way home, on a whim, decided to step into the Poetry Library. She thought it was too great a coincidence, so cleared her throat, adding that to have recognised the back of my head was proof that I had left a good impression on her.

The week before, I taught a six-day poetry course at the Arvon Centre in Lumb Bank for Apples & Snakes. To largely performance-orientated poets, I had stressed the importance of reading and publishing poetry; how it creates a legacy, a record; how others can come to your work after you pass, how when you are alive, you can travel without moving; how you become a part of something larger, historic, cartographic of British Poetry. I spoke regretfully arrogantly and patronisingly to the students and on the last night, I was brought sharply down to earth by the poet Miriam Nash. She reminded me that eight or so years before, Jacob Sam-La Rose had identical conversations with us in another Arvon Centre, deftly controlling his flabbergast that we, who had also come to poetry from performance, were not active readers.

How cyclical is the world and our times within it? The positions we play; from conflict to chaos, to conversations about poetry? Behind me are shelves and shelves of books by authors who I imagine were sat down and lectured to read poetry too; "it'll broaden your world view, your artistic impulse, your voice, your everything…" Perhaps there is another way of looking at this #*Afterhours* project. Perhaps it's also an act of honouring similar conversations that led to the publication of these books I now pore through, easily, casually selecting poems to pick apart and put back together; conversations that have happened, that will happen, that will keep on happening.

1986
Michael Hofmann

From the book *Acrimony*

ALBION MARKET

Warm air and no sun – the sky was like cardboard,
the same depthless no-colour as the pavements and buildings.
It was May, and pink cherry blossoms lay and shoaled
in the gutter, bleeding as after some wedding...

Broken glass, corrugated tin and spraygunned plywood saying
Arsenal rules the world. Twenty floors up Chantry Point,
the grey diamond panels over two arsoned windows
were scorched like a couple of raised eyebrows.

Tireless and sick, women hunted for bargains.
Gold and silver were half-price. Clothes shops
started up, enjoyed a certain vogue, then
went into a tailspin of permanent sales,

cutting their throats. A window waved *Goodbye, Kilburn,*
and *Everything Must Go.* The *Last Day* was weeks ago –
it didn't. The tailor's became *Rock Bottom.*
On the pavement, men were selling shoelaces.

A few streets away, in the renovated precinct,
girls' names and numbers stood on every lamp-post,
phone-booth, parking meter and tree. Felt tip on sticky labels,
'rubber', and 'correction' for the incorrigible.

At night, the taxis crawled through Bayswater,
where women dangled their 'most things considered' from the kerb.
A man came down the street with the meth-pink eyes
of a white rat, his gait a mortal shuffle.

A British bulldog bowler hat clung to his melting skull.
. . . Game spirits, tat and service industries,
an economy stripped to the skin trade. Sex and security,
Arsenal boot boys, white slaves and the SAS.

JENTA APTA MARKET 1986
#*After* Michael Hofmann

Warm air and stifling sun – the sky was like cardboard,
that same depthless tincture as the walls of each shack.
It was May, and one fresh mango lay stripped of flesh
in the gutters, bleeding after a battle with a child's teeth.

Broken glass, corrugated tin and painted plywood saying
Vote For Lawrence Onoja stood before baskets of tomatoes
heaped like offerings, and four floors above: two scorched
shutters perched open like palms raised in prayer. Below,

tireless, quick-witted women hunted bargains, some with
offspring who scuttled after, others alone, their swaying
hips thick music to the parched butchers and ignored
roadside cooks who cursed and grabbed at the chickens,

cutting their throats. A window waved *Goodbye, kill, burn
this sacrifice!* its glass eyes winking at suspected witches –
the silent southern women who only paid with promises,
who were shunned in public, but sought out at dusk when

a few streets away, in the renovated precinct, the police
who had added girls' names to their missing persons list,
who promised restless searches but promptly fell asleep,
stirred to seek hot dinners and to swap their last shifts.

At night, dark taxis crawled through bays. Water sloshed
from the makeshift ovens dug by the cooks, now potholes
where women knew to wait, dangling their bodily goods
to the slowing drivers. Uncle Uyi walked down this street.

A British bulldog bowler hat clung to his melting skull,
eyes red with drug addiction. Years later, we'd learn this
was when last you saw your brother, that his gait, a mortal
shuffle, echoed in mine, so you prayed, prayed and prayed.

07/01/15// Diary Entry #7

Today I'm working on the fourth poem for 1987. Last week, I searched for it by poring through the Poetry Book Society's recommendations for that year. I speed-read as many of the books as I could, making snap decisions. These are the notes I made:

***

John Ash, *Disbelief*, published by Carcanet.
Long lines, flowing thought, not necessarily narrative, the tone is more 'about' the world than it is 'of' the world. Difficult to find a poem that can frame a story about my parents. The syntax is a tad too conversational.

Charles Tomlinson, *The Return*, Oxford Poets.
Most of the poems in the collection are set in Liguria, in north-west Italy, i.e. the consciousness of the poet is elsewhere. I'm trying to make British/Irish poetic consciousness Nigerian, to travel them back through time. This would mean taking Liguria back to Nigeria – which is beyond the confines of this project. Perhaps I am clutching at straws here or it is just my instincts searching for a reason to put the book down. Also, the titles and locations do not feel easily translatable...

Ken Smith, *Wormwood*, Bloodaxe.
The poems are set in a prison and taken from Ken's experiences there, which I cannot translate or directly relate to as I have never set foot in a prison and neither have my parents. The poems are fascinating though, and such great writing.

Martin Stokes, *The First Death of Venice*, Bloodaxe.
The poems are about death, destruction and war... none of which I can situate in 1987 Nigeria or in the story of my family. I am grabbed by the poem 'Elegy for my sister' – I have a twin sister and have often wondered what might've been had she been male, if she had died at birth or if spirit-children had

claimed her. Dark thought. Besides, it is a long poem and at the moment, brevity feels prime for #*Afterhours*.

Paul Muldoon, *Meeting the British*, Faber and Faber.
As titles go, given the nature of the project, this is perfect. I find two possible poems: 'The Coney' and 'Sushi'.

Phillip Gross, *Cat's Whisker*, Faber and Faber.
I enjoy reading, find two poems that fit perfectly with themes established by the poems already written: 'English as a Foreign Language' and 'Two Waters'.

Peter Redgrove, *In the Hall of the Saurians*, Secker & Warburg.
My favourite poem is 'A Few Carats of Pain' but possible poems for #*Afterhours*: 'A Dewy Garment' and 'Concerning Dreams'.

Seamus Heaney, *The Haw Lantern*, Faber and Faber.
Of all the collections, I enjoy this the most and find three possible poems: 'From the Land of the Unspoken', 'Clearances' and 'The Shooting Script'. The first poem is so perfect and easily translatable, I can't think of what I'd need to change to make it more 'Nigerian'. I spent three years in Ireland and this poem is further proof of the similarities between the Irish and Nigerian temperament. I still write (in application forms, when I'm asked about my nationality) that a quarter of my soul is Irish. This poem suggests I have underestimated myself; I ought to write half.

***

I whittle the poems down to: 'The Coney', 'Two Waters', 'From the Land of the Unspoken' and 'The Shooting Script'. In 'The Coney', a man writes to his father. I was four at the time, so I cannot write this poem and given its drama, my father cannot write it to me. 'Two Waters' is just too close to the poem written for 1986. I need something else to happen. In 'The Land of the Unspoken', the 'I' can't be mine or my father's which leaves 'The Shooting Script'. So, this will be the poem!

22/01/15// Diary Entry #8

Today I finished 1987's poem – the fourth poem for the #*Afterhours* project. The more I read 'A Shooting Script' by Seamus Heaney, the more I loved its conceit and execution, how it doesn't tell, but shows. The poem is, as the title suggests, a script for shooting that a writer might give to a director. It details what the camera should capture and how to capture it: Ireland in the 1920s. In the first three stanzas, we see teachers cycle past members of a community that seem in harmony, at peace with each other. They salute native speakers, follow the language to conversations about translation jobs, suggesting a vibrant Ireland in transition. All this is halted in the fourth stanza by a figure adorned with a cape and biretta...

Freeze on his blank face. Let the credits run

...Seamus commands us. This is the threat, the stumbling block in the sweeping harmony of the shooting script, a defiant, unflinching, unsmiling lone figure. But there is hope, "just when it looks like it is all over..." Seamus commands the camera to find someone on a beach writing in the old Irish script, in the "running sand" – painting a very romantic and affecting ending which seems to say Irish values will live on, even as the waves crash and the ground beneath washes away.

On first reading, I thought "Cape" and "Roman collar" which the figure wears, referred to army apparel, that 'Biretta' was a gun, that there was a play on "shooting" in the title, that the poem was a critique of British Army presence in Northern Ireland when the conflicts started. I began writing my version around the idea of a Nigerian soldier or police officer (both notorious for their short tempers and lack of humour) watching teachers mingling with students in northern Nigeria, watching the various tribes and their languages mix peacefully.

However, something didn't quite work. The glove didn't fit well enough. I got to the turning point – the unsmiling figure – and found the soldier-character in my poem too... absent somehow. I re-read the stanza, unpicked and unpacked the words and realised my mistake. 'Biretta' is a square cap with three flat projections on top, worn by Roman Catholic clergymen, but 'Beretta' is the gun manufacturer. A 'Roman collar' is an item of Christian clerical clothing, and the 'cape' was attached to a 'soutane', a garment also worn by Roman Catholic priests. The unsmiling figure then is a Catholic priest and the poem is also about the religious aspect of the conflict.

Early 1980s northern Nigeria wasn't too dissimilar religiously or politically. Fundamentalist Islam was in its early stages, its influence over secular life growing more powerful. Old tribal grudges, climate change, rich Christian southern Nigerians who travelled north after the civil war created a volatile environment that eventually exploded, and is the chaos northern Nigeria finds itself in today. I chose to create a figure to embody this this, a down-and-out Muslim cattle herder, to replace Seamus's priest. I swapped Seamus's teachers for missionaries, the writing in the sand for my parents: an interfaith couple back then, navigating the world, trying to stay safe, and the poem began to work again.

1987
Seamus Heaney
From the book *The Haw Lantern*

A SHOOTING SCRIPT

They are riding away from whatever might have been
Towards what will never be, in a held shot:
Teachers on bicycles, saluting native speakers,
Treading the nineteen-twenties like the future.

Still pedalling out at the end of the lens,
Not getting anywhere and not getting away.
Mix to fuchsia that 'follows the language'.
A long soundless sequence. Pan and fade.

Then voices over, in different Irishes,
Discussing translation jobs and rates per line;
Like nineteenth-century milestones in grass verges,
Occurrence of names like R. M. Ballantyne.

A close-up on the cat's eye of a button
Pulling back wide to the cape of a soutane,
Biretta, Roman collar, Adam's apple.
Freeze his blank face. Let the credits run

And just when it looks as if it is all over –
Tracking shots of a long wave up a strand
That breaks towards the point of a stick writing and writing
Words in the old script in the running sand.

A SHOOTING SCRIPT 1987
#*After* **Seamus Heaney**

They are riding from what might have been
towards what will come to be, in a locked shot:
Missionaries on bicycles greeting Muslim boys,
priming the eighties for the troubled future,

still pedalling out at the end of the lens,
circling the teens like ambushed prey.
Mix to desert dust floating in hot breeze.
An ominous long sequence. Pan and fade.

Then voices over, of different tribal dogma,
discussing politics, failed civilian rule, the pull
of Christian capital, dwindling grazing land,
occurrence of names like Matthew and Paul.

A close-up on the cat's eye of a white button
pulling back wide to a kaftan, black turban,
rifle, parched fields, herd of starving cattle.
Freeze his livid face. Let the credits run.

And just when it looks as if it is all over –
tracking shots of a mosque, the muezzin stands
for the call to prayer, sings over the young
interfaith couple washing off their hands.

1988
Jo Shapcott
From the book *Electroplating the Baby*

PHOTOGRAPH: SHEEPSHEARING
Northlew, 1917

Here are six men, their tools, a cart,
a hedge with three trees breaking its smooth line.
Only half the men actually shear:
they have such control over those raggy piles
of sheep that they can still sustain
a hard stare out at us – not the modern, ironic
glance to camera, but a single-minded look
held for the full seconds needed to etch the image
on the photographic plate. In this way
they have looked themselves into my sphere.
Two boys man the hand-wound wheels
which drive the clippers. A tricky role:
to pose, frozen, while giving the impression
of vigorous wheel-turning. One is better at it.
The sixth character is the youngest boy.
He holds a sheep jammed against his upper legs,
its head in one hand, rump in the other.
This sheep will be the next for the clippers.
The anxiety of the two – the one for the shearing
of her fleece, the other for the enormity of his task
of staying stock-still for history –
is palpable in this one surprising
blur of fleece and features in the scene.
It is a fuzz of boy and sheep to set your teeth on edge:
a vibration to travel down to the bone.

PHOTOGRAPH: RAM SACRIFICING 1998

Numan, 1988

#*After* Jo Shapcott

Here are four men, their knives, a rope,
a gutter with sludge slow-moving through its gut.
Only one man will actually cut:
One has such control over those rugged rippled
horns that he can still sustain
a hard stare out at us – not the modern, staged
suave selfie but a single-minded look
held for the second needed to burn the image
on the photographic film. In this way
he looks himself into my future.
Two boys man the four hoofs tied together,
the rope biting through hide. A tricky role:
to straddle, to pose, while giving the impression
the bucking beast is still. One is better at it.
The fourth character, the youngest boy, is me.
He rests a foot on the ram's throat,
a knife in one hand, uncle's hand in the other.
This ram will be next for the sacrifice.
The anxiety of the two – the one as offering
to God, the other for the enormity of the task
of Eid's ritual slaughter –
is pumping in this one surprising
shot of knives and horns in this scene.
It is a flash of boy and beast to set your teeth on edge:
a slide to cut down to the bone.

19/02/15 // Diary Entry #10

Today, 1989's poem, the sixth one for *#Afterhours*, will either be 'Girl' by Simon Armitage or 'Writ in Water' by Charles Boyle. I'd like to write about the birth of my little sister and what impact it had on my five-year-old mind. Part of the *#Afterhours* residency involves writing about the library and those who use the space, about *#PoetryLibraryPeople*.

I meet Dmitry. A soft-spoken, silver-ringed, green-scarved, slim-built, lightly greying man who isn't here for the poetry but to escape the noisy children and everyone else in the Southbank Centre. I ask if he has an interest in poetry and he replies he enjoys it, a bit, but isn't an avid reader. *I have an interest*, he says, *my earliest memory is at school, we had to learn poems off by heart.* Really? I ask, *Yes, we have to do that in Russia – I'm Russian – and we had to recite it out loud in the mornings. It's a great way to train your memory, so you see, Russians are full of poetry.* What kind of poems? *Pushkin's fairy tales, I knew them off by heart. In fact...* he says, slipping into nostalgia, warmth coming to his voice, *I knew them better than my grandmother who taught them to me. I'd get her to recite them and correct her mistakes, ha!* Have you read any of the poems in translation? In English? *No, it's very poetic, very difficult to translate, I don't think it is possible, you see, Pushkin is our Shakespeare, he is all about the metre, all about the rhyme, so difficult to translate, perfect all the time.*

1989
Charles Boyle

From the book *The Best of Poetry London*
(Poetry and Prose, 1988-2013)

WRIT IN WATER

Across from our office was another
like ours, but whose whole façade
was made of glass. No pane was
exactly true, and on clear mornings our late
arrivals, hangovers, feet
on desks and industrious moments
were reflected there as if in water.

Later, when they switched on their lights,
the glass gave way
like the front of an old dolls' house.
There were the serious men in suits
and the secretaries at their keyboards,
and the man who clears memos from out-trays
to distribute to in-trays.

A vent at the top uttered steam and,
one day in early spring, a brimming froth of suds
which the lightest breeze creamed off.

WRIT IN WATER & BLOOD 1989
#*After* Charles Boyle

We'd find her across from our bedroom: another
like us, but Hadiza's young skin was a translucent façade
like tracing paper or frosted glass. No pain was
light enough to pinch with, to consider, to contemplate.
Instantly, she'd begin howling around our feet,
staring up at us, replaying the small-fisted moments
of our wickedness, her face streaked with water.

Later, when Mum would switch off the room lights
to nurse her in the dark, the howls would fall away
like young skin. Silence would re-enter the house.
Dad would change from the man always in suits
to a human play-thing, a cave of flesh, a surf board
bound by blood (net of fingers, arms forming trays)
to float her towards the bathtub's warm sprays.

Once, breeze blew through a gap in the door and
cleared the steam so we'd recall the froth of suds;
what it felt to be vulnerable and taken care off.

What it felt to be vulnerable and taken care off
cleared the steam so we'd recall the froth of suds.

Once breeze blew through a gap in the door, and
to float her towards the bathtub's warm sprays,
(bound by blood, net of fingers, arms forming trays)
a human play-thing, a cave of flesh, a surf board
– Dad, would change from the serious man in suits
to young skin. Silence would re-enter the house
to nurse her. In the dark, the howls would fall away.

Later, when Mum would switch off the room-lights
of our wickedness – her face streaked with water,
staring up at us, replaying the small-fisted moments,
instantly, she'd begin howling. Around our feet:
light; enough to pinch with, to consider, to contemplate,
like tracing paper or frosted glass. No pain was
like us, but Hadiza's young skin was a translucent façade –
we'd find her across from our bedroom: another.

18/03/15// Diary Entry #11

Today I began working on the seventh poem of the #*Afterhours* project and the poem I will rework is 'Transformers' by Robert Crawford. It tells a childhood story of playing with model trains around Pictish Stones. A Pictish Stone is a type of stone monument usually carved or incised with symbols or designs. There are four trains mentioned in the poem: Ivanhoe, The Lady of the Lake, The Fair Maid of Perth and Royal Scotsman (referred to as Royal Scots). They all operated in Scotland, steaming through the Highlands. All of them, save Royal Scots, were titles of poems or stories by Sir Walter Scott, and Royal Scots was also the King of Scotland's army. As the voice in the poem plays, he/she catches the other trains falling off the Pictish stones, but forgets Royal Scots in the grass. The poem ends... "Mist was perforated with cries and grinding metal. Royal Scots poured from the stones".

Sir Walter Scott was the first English-language author to have a truly international career in his life time, and Robert's lines half way through the poem; "I laid them [the trains] in the loft, peering at them, wondering if they'd work on my layout" suggests a struggle with making these objects fit in the world of the poem. Going symbolism-crazy, perhaps the struggle is of English/expansion/industrialisation/military power etc., fitting in the Scottish world... in which case, at the end, where the Royal Scots pours from the stones, means something... heavier.

To hazard a guess, I'd say the poem is deeply about Scottish military independence, about identity and sacrifice. I still have no clue how it is linked to 'Transformers' as a title. I think of Transformers, the toys produced by the Japanese company Takara, to an American toy company Hasbro, which got the CGI/live action/cinematic treatment, which Michael Bay destroyed in the last instalment. I think of a simple electrical current, how a transformer is a device that transfers electric energy between two circuits, and if a circuit is broken, the device dies. I wonder who or what might have died in Robert's life.

I love this poem, but the only steer I have towards rewriting is to think of Chinua Achebe, the first English-language African author to have a truly international career in his lifetime, and I wonder if I can take some of his titles as a starting point for my poem.

1990
Robert Crawford
From the book *A Scottish Assembly*

TRANSFORMER

Lengths of model railway track jutted from the Pictish stones.
When I bent down to look at a horseman's head or at the comb
and mirror, scale-model engines hurtled towards me. *Ivanhoe,
The Lady of the Lake, The Fair Maid of Perth* with gleaming
pistons – I had to catch them or they'd shoot off the ends of
their tracks. I lurched from stone to stone, grabbing them. In
the darkness they slackened off. At midnight I wrapped the
locomotives in plastic bags to carry them away; their metal
bodies grew heavy and cold as I walked. Home, I laid them
in the loft, peering at them, wondering if they'd work on my
layout. That night I saw them carved new, crewed by warriors,
steaming their way into battle. At Aberlemno model replica
carriages with Victorian coachwork lay in the grass, unspotted.
Mist was perforated with cries and grinding metal. *Royal Scots*
poured from the stones.

TRANSFORMER 1990
#After **Robert Crawford**

Falling asleep on the bumpy road from our house to Kano airport, I woke to look down at the familiar cracked earth, instead, smooth tarmac beneath jet engines hurtled towards me. *No longer at ease,* the plane rose like *An Arrow of God* over *Anthills of the Savannah* – our neighbourhoods below, sprawled out, naked and unprotected. I panicked, believed I had to watch both wings or they'd shoot off the sides of the plane. I struggled inside the seatbelt's grip to grab what glimpse I could, till darkness swallowed the whole world and I tired of worrying. Later, I laid down on a kitchen floor, my small self pressed to the hard tiles, peering at them, grateful for the stiff surety. That night I saw them spread across waters, crews of workmen from Constantine to Marseille, from where my continent met the Mediterranean and disappeared, to surface after miles of water. Mist parted in intervals, I saw for the first time *An Image Of Africa* and lost it instantly, among the clouds.

01/04/15 // Diary Entry #12

Yesterday, General Buhari was elected president of Nigeria. In 1984, when I was born, he was also the head of state, though he assumed power by military coup. He enforced a dictatorial style of governance where folks were imprisoned for speaking against his government and for misdemeanours, like being unruly in queues. Some were forced to do push-ups as punishment. Buhari swears he is a changed man now, and evidently many Nigerians believe this to be true.

The same sense of chaos and impending change I felt during the Nigerian election, I feel as we lead up to England's general election. I held my breath for Nigeria and after a brief exhale, I am about to do the same for England. This is sometimes what it feels like seeking poems for #*Afterhours*. Soon after completing a response/rewrite, I begin again, wondering whose voice to trust, which to elect to govern my emotions and thoughts, if its structures, systems and spirits match mine, and if I trust it, it will serve me well.

For 1991, by flicking through the Poetry Book Society's recommendations for 1991 and discounting those from other countries, I'm left with books by Sarah Maguire, Jackie Kay and Helen Dunmore. I find Helen's poems in *Short Days, Long Nights*, to be the most entertaining, her imagery, line breaks and ideas constantly surprising, inventive and gasp-out-loud-good. I have to hush myself a few times as I read, I fear scaring others in the library. The most moving and emotionally-charged poems were found in Jackie's *Adoption Papers*, which tell the story of discovering her birth, and employs her and her mother's voices. I love the poems, but cannot think of a way of rewriting any, as none of her family's dynamics exist in mine. Sarah Maguire's *Spilt Milk*, the last to read, is perfect. Kayo Chingonyi, poet and good friend, randomly passing through the library, peeks over my shoulder and smiles warmly "Mmm, that's a good book".

In 1991, my family and I travelled around a bit within Nigeria and internationally. We lived for a short while in Lagos, and this is what I'd like to write about. Perfectly, Sarah has a poem called 'Moving Home', another called 'Cherry Tree' (which I could use to write about the mango tree we found growing in the backyard of the house we stayed in) and a long poem called 'Still At Sea' which is also perfect and thematically follows on from 1990's poem. In that poem, I wrote about first flying over the Mediterranean Sea and dreaming about it. Sarah's poems begins...

Each night you returned
to the Mediterranean...

To return to electoral language, Sarah has my vote.

1991
Sarah Maguire
From the book *Spilt Milk*

STILL AT SEA

Each night you returned
to the Mediterranean
just touching Marsala

and would dream of the sea
repeating itself,
the light slivering

all over your ceiling.
Each night you woke
with his back humped

against yours, his fists
gripping the pillows,
as he dreamt of his cargoes

packed in dry docks,
or of the Caspian Sea
locked into itself.

Then, after half a life,
you left his house
full of maps and dust

and found your paints
in thirteen shades
of cobalt blue and jade.

In Cefalù your dream
became your home:
a house on the harbour

where the sea slapped
at your walls.
Standing in the kitchen,

up to your elbows
in underwear and soap,
you would look out

to find the waves
organising the pebbles,
scouring the rocks.

At night, alone
with the moonlight
and a smallish grappa,

you pictured yourself
as a Cubist sacrifice:
sectioned in monochrome,

your lap full of triangles,
the moon shifting
her perspectives

to whiten your ankles,
throw your mouth into
doubt. You occupied

that house nine months –
watching the seasons,
then the tourists,

come and go. Each morning
there was coffee and
fresh foccaccia by the sea,

then the market for
your aubergines and fennel,
or that blue and silver

banded fish; once home
you'd take a knife and slit
it up the belly to reveal

the sack of wasted eggs,
the liver, then the tiny heart:
its carmine blood

releasing the grain
of your scrubbed deal table
and its memories of leaves.

Three years' silence
and I wonder
if you're still at sea.

I spread out
all your letters on my desk
to plot your travels:

they're full of water-colours –
mostly harbours,
reaching out to light.

The very last
tells how you found
the cigarette machine

outside your door split
by a bullet-hole,
its fractured glass

like the sun a child might draw
on the edge of a tablecloth.
There was no blood

to be seen: only the smell
of washed stone,
and a woman with a bucket

slipping out of view.

STILL AT SEA 1991
#*After* Sarah Maguire

Each night, you returned
to the Mediterranean
just touching Marseille

and would dream of the sea,
its rough surface tiled
smooth by the workmen

you'd draw at the table,
each diligently clicking
into place the baked earth.

Against your father's wishes,
I'd watch you gripping pillows
as you dreamt of drowning –

packed as you were
between the sheets,
locked inside yourself.

Then in the morning
you'd leave to school
full of maps and tremors

and find your classmates
too risible, too confident
in soil's surety.

In Ajao Estate, your dream
engulfed our new home:
a house by the airport

where the sky's roar
shook the windows.
Standing by the kitchen sink

in your soaked shirt,
up to your elbows in soap
you would look out

to find the clouds
hiding the planes,
cloaking their descent.

At night, alone
with the moonlight
and a smallish sketchpad,

you pictured yourself
a maverick architect
reconstructing Atlantis,

your lap full of rulers,
the moon shifting
her deposition

to whiten your ankles,
throw a ghostly sheen
over you. It occupied

you for months;
watching the skies shift,
those aircrafts come

and go. Each morning
there were grid lines
erased from the sea

you had painted, proof
you distrusted your attempts
at safe passage,

as if in your dreams,
walking among the waves
and workmen, a plane lost

its wings, crashed through
your foundations, drowning
the passengers.

Bodies surfaced, faces
frozen, mouths agape,
eyes like soaked moons,

teeth jeweling
dark skin dissolving
to suffocating darkness.

Three years of silence
before you found
adequate words to tell, years

where I'd spread out
your drawings on the floor
to guess at your thoughts,

scrubbing your scribbles off
the walls, for them to reappear
days later, haunting us

scarring the surface,
deep, violent,
compulsive slashes

like how a child might score
the edge of a table
when no one was there

to rebuke: only the smell
of scrubbed tiles
and a mother with a bucket

slipping out of view.

15/04/15// Diary Entry #13

To this day, the Director of the National Theatre of Libya calls me a "Gaddafi Supporter". We met at a breakfast table a few years ago, shortly before a book festival in Tripoli. It was the first festival since the fall of Gaddafi and I was invited to read poems, talk about being a published poet and about my work in theatre. Breakfast was in the hotel I stayed at, where during the night we'd hear rapid gunfire and watch car chases through the streets, tyres skidding in the engine smoke and moonlight. In the morning, we'd explore the bullet holes in the walls and gather spent shells. Heavily-armed French and American security detail, contracted to guard oil fields and refineries, breakfasted with us, guns glinting among the croissants and fresh orange juice. Months later, I'd learn that the entire front of the building was rocketed by rebels, smoked out, destroyed, but at the time it was peaceful and I was standing my ground about Colonel Gaddafi. The Director thought I was crazy.

I still stand my ground about Gaddafi. One of the reasons is a poem by Simon Armitage, called 'Poem'. You can find it online. I love its deceptive simplicity, its authentic balance, and how it perfectly paints a picture of a human being. During breakfast it was on my mind. My intention was and still is to write a poem *after* this about Gaddafi; to show how he did horrible things, but also the most incredible things for his land and for his people, with more incredible pan-African plans in the works before his eventful dethronement and murder. I explained my intentions to the Director and he said he'd consider publishing it; I should send it when it is ready.

'Poem' was published in 1992, in Armitage's *Kid*, which I reread this morning looking for a poem for #*Afterhours*. I rediscovered 'Not The Furniture Game'. For poets who work in education, this poem is a gift that keeps giving. It is boundlessly inventive and energetic, kids dig the language and the turn at the end. It is perfect for *#Afterhours*. I can stick closely to its structure, yet write whatever the hell I want.

I want to write about malaria, how it affected my mother and how that affected us in 1992.

1992
Simon Armitage
From the book *Kid*

NOT THE FURNITURE GAME

His hair was a crow fished out of a blocked chimney
and his eyes were boiled eggs with the tops hammered in
and his blink was a cat flap
and his teeth were bluestones or Easter Island statues
and his bite was a perfect horseshoe.
His nostrils were both barrels of a shotgun, loaded.
And his mouth was an oil exploration project gone bankrupt
and his last smile was a caesarean section
and his tongue was an iguanodon
and his whistle was a laser beam
and his laugh was a bad case of kennel cough.
He coughed, and it was malt whisky.
And his headaches were Arson in Her Majesty's Dockyards
and his arguments were outboard motors strangled with fishing-line
and his neck was a bandstand
and his Adam's apple was a ball cock
and his arms were milk running off from a broken bottle.
His elbows were boomerangs or pinking shears.
And his wrists were ankles
and his handshakes were puff adders in the bran tub
and his fingers were astronauts found dead in their spacesuits
and the palms of his hands were action paintings
and both thumbs were blue touchpaper.
And his shadow was an opencast mine.
And his dog was a sentry-box with no one in it
and his heart was a first world war grenade discovered by children
and his nipples were timers for incendiary devices
and his shoulder-blades were two butchers at the meat-cleaving
    competition

and his belly-button was the Falkland Islands
and his private parts were the Bermuda triangle
and his backside was a priest hole
and his stretchmarks were the tide going out.
The whole system of his blood was Dutch elm disease.
And his legs were depth charges
and his knees were fossils waiting to be tapped open
and his ligaments were rifles wrapped in oilcloth under the
    floorboards
and his calves were the undercarriages of Shackletons.
The balls of his feet were where meteorites had landed
and his toes were a nest of mice under the lawn-mower.
And his footprints were Vietnam
and his promises were hot-air balloons floating off over the trees
and his one-liners were footballs through other people's windows
and his grin was the Great Wall of China as seen from the moon
and the last time they talked, it was apartheid.

She was a chair, tipped over backwards
with his donkey jacket on her shoulders.

They told him,
and his face was a hole
where the ice had not been thick enough to hold her.

NOT THE FURNITURE GAME 1992

or *Portrait of my mother with malaria*

#After **Simon Armitage**

Her hair was a gnarled bush of scorched Bible pages
and her eyes were halves of guava fruit rotten at the edges
and her blink was a white flag
and her teeth were headstones or flat cowrie shells
and her bite was a soft u-turn.
Her nostrils were open beaks of twin hatchlings, hungry.
And her mouth was a village well, long dried out
and her last smile was a vasectomy
and her tongue was a soiled rag
and her whistle was a wilting leaf
and her laugh was a mild case of whooping cough.
She coughed, and it was a stew of bitter herbs.
And her headaches were fires in the president's chambers
and her arguments were clumps of grass hurled at churning blades
and her neck was a rubber band
and her throat was a wet road
and her arms were chopped boiled okra oozing from a pot.
Her elbows were corn stalks or plantain peels.
And her wrists were limp anchors
and her handshakes were earthworms in lightly salted water
and her fingers were washwomen found dead in the river
and the palms of her hands were tragic poems
and both thumbs were small candles.
And her shadow was a mourner's veil.
And her cat was a sandbox with no one near it
and her heart was a Biafran war hip-flask discovered by orphans
and her nipples were corks for medicinal containers
and her shoulder-blades were wet nurses at a refugee camp
and her belly-button was Soweto

and her private parts were The Sudan
and her backside was a borehole
and her stretchmarks were the start of desertification.
The whole system of her blood was a hairline fracture.
And her legs were hose pipes
and her knees were gnarled roots soaked to be softened
and her ligaments were bristles wrapped in baking paper
and her calves were the upturned bellies of beached fish.
The balls of her feet were where top soil eroded
and her toes were parched slugs seeking shade.
And her footprints were Rwanda
and her promises were thin jewels forged in the dark
and her one-liners were arrows fallen short of their target
and her grin was a border-line seen from six feet below
and the last time we talked it was a famine.

We were a riot, spilling across streets
with her to fan whenever fires were lit.

We were told,
and our faces became rubble
where the stone facade fell unable to hold her weight.

Doodle - 1993

1993
Moniza Alvi
From the book *Split World: Poems 1990-2005*

MAP OF INDIA

If I stare at the country long enough
I can prise it off the paper,
lift it like a flap of skin.

Sometimes it's an advent calendar –
each city has a window
which I leave open
a little wider each time.

India is manageable – smaller than
my hand, the Mahanadi River
thinner than my lifeline.

MAP OF NIGERIA 1993
#*After* Moniza Alvi

If I stare at Africa long enough
I can prize it off the paper,
lift it like a flag of skin.

Sometimes it's gun-shaped –
each country conducive
to the solid dark weight
I imagine balanced perfectly.

Nigeria guards the trigger – larger than
most, the Niger River – the hairline,
longer than my lifeline.

06/05/15// Diary Entry #15

The last two weeks have been pretty exciting for *#Afterhours*. I was interviewed on BBC Radio 3's flagship poetry show *The Verb*, by the incomparable Ian McMillan, where I talked about the poems thus far. I asked my twitter followers for suggestions and, Ian actually choose the poem for 1993, 'Map of India' by Moniza Alvi. I completed my version 'Map of Nigeria' the following week and last Tuesday, was fortunate enough to bump into Moniza at the launch of Mona Arshi's book *Small Hands*. Mona had been tutored by Moniza, who was delighted when I told her about the re-writing of her poem. Today, I must begin searching for the poem for 1994.

To shake things up, I try another approach. Instead of using solely the *Poetry Book Society* recommendations as a source, I reach for *Poetry Review* magazines published in 1994, and stumble across 1994's New Generation Poets... and chuckle, thinking that some of these poets, incredibly established now, were once 'new'. Selected once every decade, the list of the haloed twenty reads:

Moniza Alvi
Simon Armitage
John Burnside
Robert Crawford
David Dabydeen
Michael Donaghy
Carol Ann Duffy
Ian Duhig
Elizabeth Garrett
Lavinia Greenlaw
W.N. Herbert
Michael Hoffman
Mick Imlah

Kathleen Jamie
Sarah Maguire
Glyn Maxwell
Jamie McKendrick
Don Paterson
Pauline Stainer
Susan Wicks

No less that sixty percent of the poems already completed for #*Afterhours* are in response to six of these poets. When 2014's Next Generation Poets list was released, my ridiculous disappointment at not being selected disappeared within seconds of noticing neither had any of my poetry heroes. I railed against the list on that basis for about a day and half, then simply let it go. Elsewhere, tempers flared. There were four-letter-word-littered Facebook rants, discussions, debates and counter lists constructed... which only served to make me think critically about those selected. I looked through them again... Tara Bergin, Emily Berry, Sean Borodale, Adam Foulds, Annie Freud, Alan Gillis, Rebecca Goss, Jen Hadfield, Emma Jones, Luke Kennard, Melissa Lee-Houghton, Hannah Lowe, Kei Miller, Helen Mort, Daljit Nagra, Heather Phillipson, Kate Tempest, Mark Waldron, Sam Willetts and Jane Yeh... and realised how healthy and diverse it was, that I personally knew more than half of the poets on the list, that I liked and respected their work... and that if the 1994 lot, who are so established now were selected similarly, then one can't fault the process.

The task at hand is still to pick a 1994 poem and combining The Next Generation with the Poetry Book Society recommendations, I discover that 1994 was an astonishing year for poetry, with books by Duncan Bush, George Charlton, Peter Didsbury, W.N. Herbert, Gerard Woodward, Hugo Williams, John Burnside, Tom Paulin and Iain Crichton Smith. I try my method of speed-reading and snap decision-making, but so good are the books and the poems that I'm forced to slow down and devour, promising to return in future when I have more time to spare. I whittle the books down to Peter, John, Tom and Duncan, but in the final hours of the day, return to first poem I thought perfect: 'The King and Queen of Dumfriesshire' by W.N. Herbert.

Bill Herbert aka W.N. Herbert was my mentor during the year-long Complete Works poetry project designed by Dr Nathalie Teitler and Bernardine Evaristo. Mona Arshi was one of us, and though not a little nepotism is at play here, his poem, inspired by a statue of the same name in Scotland, is a portrait of a couple's domestic disharmony and is perfect for what I hope to write about: domestic disharmony in a boarding school in Nigeria. In 1994, my twin sister and I joined Federal Government College Odogbolu, and that first night away from home, in the cavernous dining hall, a fight started when a senior female student broke a glass bottle across the face of a senior male student. This is where I will start my poem.

1994
W. N. Herbert

From the book *Cabaret McGonagall*

THE KING AND QUEEN OF DUMFRIESSHIRE

The King and Queen of Dumfriesshire sit
in their battery-dead Triumph, gazing ahead
at an iced-over windscreen like a gull rolled flat.
They are cast in bronze, with Henry Moore holes
shot in each other by incessant argument;
these are convenient for holding her tartan flask,
his rolled-up *Scotsman*. The hairy skeleton
of a Border terrier sits in the back window,
not nodding. On the back seat rests
their favourite argument, the one about
how he does not permit her to see the old friends
she no longer likes and he secretly misses;
the one which is really about punishing each other
for no longer wanting to make love.
The argument is in the form of a big white bowl
with a black band around it hand-painted with fruit.
It has a gold rim, and in it lies
a brown curl of water from the leaking roof.
Outside, the clouds continue
to bomb the glen with sheep, which bare
their slate teeth as they tumble,
unexpectedly sneering.
The King and Queen of Dumfriesshire sit
like the too-solid bullet-ridden ghosts
of Bonny and Clyde, not eating their
tinned salmon sandwiches, crustless, still
wrapped in tinfoil, still in the tupperware.
They survey their domain, not glancing at
each other, not removing from the glove compartment
any of the old words they have always used
to keep their only threat at bay: of separation.

THE KING AND QUEEN OF ODOGBOLU, 1994
#*After* **W.N. Herbert.**

The head boy and girl, King and Queen of Odogbolu sit
in the vast dim-lit boarding school hall, gazing ahead
at us johnny-just-comes, numb from the shock. *So flat*
they're all concave! they laugh and point, firing holes,
shots through our shredded confidence. An argument
(these will become the norm) erupts to a riot. A flask
hisses over, ruptures against a wall and I am a skeleton
of rigid fear scanning for my sister. There's a window,
not running like other first years, her shoulders rest
their blades against its pane and I hurl a prayer about
how wings come to those who wait, past new friends.
She doesn't hear it. The hallowed lift of my voice misses
the mark of her among the stampede, falls to another
fortunate to be hoisted out and I wonder if this is Love.

The argument spills crude-oil-like; an upturned bowl
with dark thickenings: small vicious bursts like sick fruit,
its rising violent wave to peak, to collapse where she lies –
a thin brown defiant thing, her eyes raised to the roof.
Outside, the night skies reflect what I'm feeling, continue
to shift and part for blossoming old memories to bare
their emotional truths: Love? Was it? When she'd tumble
unexpectedly off her bicycle – the other kids sneering?
The head boy and girl, King and Queen of Odogbolu, sit
like weakening spirits, the stampede slowing to ghosts
off-colour: thrones over a blurring world – *Love?* Their
tin-crown influence failing – *Is this Love?* I'm asking, still
wrapped in its scope and the King and Queen are unaware.
They survey their domain but cannot glance beneath at
each first year's heart, at how vast its compartment,
at the many of the ways we'll rise against them, how Love is used
to form new worlds, even tonight, our first of separation.

03/06/15// Diary Entry #16

The last poem was difficult to write. I set myself the task of using the start *and* end words of each line from 'The King and Queen of Dumfriesshire' by W.N. Herbert, as the start and end words in my poem. It worked and I enjoyed the enormity of the challenge, but I will never, NEVER do that again. I think.

I have been on the road for the last two weeks and I am set to be on the road for the next two, travelling to Paris and Madrid consecutively to hold Midnight Runs – more of this later. Today, I set myself the task of looking for two poems: one for 1995 and 1996, and I find them almost immediately. It usually takes two days to find one; two in less than an hour is a record. I find them tucked into a *Poetry Review* magazine (Spring 1995) and *The Best of Poetry London, (Poetry and Prose, 1988 - 2013)*. The poems are 'Life Sentence' by Elizabeth Bartlett and 'The Ecstasy of St Saviours Avenue' by Neil Rollinson. I want to write about the death of the Nigerian writer and environmental activist Ken Saro-Wiwa in 1995, and about leaving Nigeria in 1996. Both are rather heavy topics and the poems by these two fine poets are perfect, they have such space for interpretation. 'Life Sentence' is about a woman poised to be executed (as Ken was) and 'The Ecstasy of St Saviours Avenue', though it is about coitus on a Valentine's night, I am confident I can make about discovering a new city, about childhood innocence and let a bit of the coitus back in... but first, Ken.

Ken is a legendary figure in Nigeria and across the world. Many believe his death was orchestrated by the oil company Shell and the corrupt Nigerian government at the time led by president Sani Abacha. He is a martyr to many and inspiration to those fighting environmental causes. He is all these to me. He is also the father of my friends, his twin daughters, Noo and Zina. They are great, great people and in 2012, to ready myself to visit Nigeria 16 years after I left, I read Noo's magnificent travelog *Looking for Transwonderland: Travels in Nigeria*. Decades after her family fled, the book details her return visit. The pages where she describes reclaiming and reassembling her father's bones on a table, to check every part of him had been collected in order to give a proper burial, is to put it most mildly, harrowing.

Years before I met Noo and Zina, Nii Parkes of Flipped Eye published *Dance The Guns to Silence*, an anthology of poems about Ken Saro-Wiwa and those executed with him. It is among the Poetry Library's collection (of course) and it has contributions from incredible writers like Chris Abani, Amiri Baraka, Kamau Braithwaite, Jayne Cortez, Fred D'Aguair, Kwame Dawes, Martin Espada and Linton Kwesi Johnson, and this is just the first half of the book! I went to the launch in London ten years ago and I return to it again. I think of his daughters, who I was ten years ago, and who I was twenty years ago, then begin writing.

1995
Elizabeth Bartlett

From the book *Appetites of Love*

LIFE SENTENCE

*'It often happens that dreams manifest an extraordinary
powerof maintaining themselves in memory.'*

The judge and jury assembled in the hours
between two and dawn, looming over the bed
where the prisoner turned and woke and feared
they could condemn her and cut off her head.

She thought the crime was infanticide or murder,
but, dazed by clips of film, muddle and confusion
surrounded everything. She picked up broken toys
and ran from her tormentors, confessed to collusion

with some partner, who was wearing the wrong face
over his old school tie and frowning slightly
as he gave his evidence that she was really
Lady MacBeth and not to be taken lightly.

Diligently scrubbing at her palm, she saw crowds
muttering in corners, but denied that she was ill
in any way or suffered from delusions of reference
or beamed on to rays which could slowly kill.

They changed the charges frequently to evade
the themes of disappointment, guilt and shame,
and bribed witnesses to affirm that she had
substituted fake stances, using another name.

And so she woke, and found it was only a dream,
as all good children's stories end to explain
why toys come to life from boxes and baskets,
but the sentence was one of life and endless pain.

Stepping into down-trodden slippers she felt
that the dream would stay with her all day.
The courtroom shadowed every door and corner
like a double exposure which would not go away.

LIFE SENTENCE 1995
For Ken Saro-Wiwa
#*After* **Elizabeth Bartlett**

The judge and junta who had stirred in the small hours
before, hugged their illicit thin gifts and stayed in bed
trying not to dream of the prisoner, how he feared
more for his land and people than he did for his head,

how his punishment would not fit his crime. No Murder
had been committed by him; the chaos and confusion
he'd caused were peaceful protest's kind. "We were toys
to them, they're done playing now". He knew collusion

was likely – that the country's corridors of power faced
the oil company's and what connected them – the slightly
greying sludge water – would burst its banks, that really,
it would become a sloe-black flood. Yet, he'd rise lightly

to the hangman who would lift the noose. No crowds
would bay, no family present, no wife wailing. No ill
willed towards the hangman, no insulting reference
to his tribe; to Ken's last few seconds they wouldn't kill

his inner gentleman. Three chances they'd have to evade
execution, thrice the trapdoor failed, thrice the shame
of noosing his clean neck. The fourth time, they'd have
it working, pulling the lever down, calling out his name.

And waking, they would wish it had all been a dream,
and try as they might, they would not be able to explain
away what sacred thing they broke, why fishing baskets
now came up slick and empty, what brand of pain

it was, how crude and sinister, how troubled they felt to have framed and killed him in the broad light of day. That courtroom would shadow every door and corner like an all-powerful omen. It would not go away.

16/07/15// Diary Entry #17

The poem I chose for 1996 is called 'The Ecstasy of St Saviours Avenue' by Neil Rollinson. 1996 is the year I left Nigeria for England and my poem will be called 'The Ecstasy of Emery Hill Street', which is where I first lived in London. I've chosen to use the first two words of each line from his poem as the first two words of mine, thus my poem begins:

> Tonight the block of flats will be called home
> and sea men we flew over precious memory.
> The windows are dark mirrors I lean against
> to cool my throbbing head and a lingering fear
> issues from where I thought myself fearless...

That last line may change... Now, part of the #*Afterhours* residency involves writing about the library and people who use the space, about #*PoetryLibraryPeople*. This is about Ron.

I met Ron here earlier this year and we viciously become fast friends. His encyclopaedic knowledge of poetry, his passion for the world of it, his unabashed love for the Poetry Library is so abundant I'm threatened by him. This is not to talk of his incredible book *Reliquaria,* his reputation in American poetry, and his growing one in Britain. He lives and lectures at NYU, but is here for a couple of years. Just to interview him, even informally as this, I feel like I gotta come correct, I gotta ask good questions.

Ron, what is the last poem you read that made want to stop writing?
> *Hmmmn... 'Frederick Douglass' by Robert Hayden.*

Why?
> *The poem did everything that a poem needed doing... it is a sonnet that defies all the rules of the sonnet... It keeps the 14*

line structure... roughly, the turning points... there are internal rhymes within it rather than end rhymes... but it goes beyond that... it does what my heart and head would want a poem to do...

What do you mean?

It is mindful of the world, of poetry, of measured hope... it begins with 'When' which isn't a conditional, but FEELS like a conditional because of the subject matter... it is playing with itself... the poem specifies the when... that fourth line where it talks about the diastole and systole, measuring the pumping of blood, of freedom become innate, a feral instinctive thing... the poem conveys something as infinite as freedom using something as formulaic and conventional as a sonnet... it is proof that we can mutiny against the thing that still gives us shape... this poem inhabits its confines yet elbows and pushes out... it is the paradox of admiration in poetry: it makes you think 'I could never do that' yet want to pick up a pen and work again... I don't think I could write something that inhabits its form and context like this... if I ever do, I will never want to write again... yet I will.

When has it meant the most to you?

I used to read that at rallies around Obama's campaign trail... it felt like we were reaching for something intangible and above us... we got it and then realised we hadn't... nowadays I think what can it mean to read a poem like this, built on the backs of men like Douglass... what does it mean for me to read this as the son of an immigrant... what does it mean to read this now as an American... ten years ago, if you had asked me this question, I would have said Prufrock or something by Edna St Vincent Millay... but this is what I keep coming to. "This man, this Douglass..."

1996
Neil Rollinson
From the book *A Spillage of Mercury*

THE ECSTASY OF ST SAVIOURS AVENUE
(Valentine's Night)

Tonight the tenement smells of oysters
and semen, chocolate and rose petals.
The windows of every flat are open
to cool us, the noise of our limberings
issues from every sash as if the building
was hyperventilating in the cold
February air. We can hear the moans
of the Rossiters, the Hendersons,
the babysitters in number 3; a gentle
pornography rousing us like an aphrodisiac.
For once the house is harmonious, we rock
in our beds; our rhythms hum
in the stone foundations.
                    We shall have to be careful;
like soldiers who must break step on a bridge.
We stagger our climaxes one by one,
from the basement flat to the attic room,
a pounding of mattresses moves through the house
in a long, multiple, communal orgasm.
The building sighs like a whorehouse.
We lie in our sheets watching the glow
of street lights colour the sky; the chimneys
blow their smoke like the mellow exhalations
of post-coital cigarettes.

THE ECSTASY OF EMERY HILL STREET 1996
(First Night in England)
#*After* Neil Rollinson

Tonight the block of flats will be called home
and sea men we flew over, memory. Through
the windows, the street light kneads my head
to cool its throbbing brain and a pulsing fear
issues from everywhere within as if my soul
was hyperventilating. I'm anxious of the cold
February air – though it is July – frightened
of the coming winter's snow, of frostbite and
the babysitters Mother might hire, of bullies,
pornography on TV; *such evil to look out for*,
for once, after reading a *Daily Mail*, sheltered
in our backyard in Nigeria as I was, I believed
in the Devil, and Great Britain his playing field.
                         We shall have to be careful
like soldiers, I warn my sisters, *tread lightly*,
we stagger our comings and goings, we run
from the kids with skin-heads, and if there is
a pounding of boots, one deep voice roaring
in a hail of sirens, it is the police: trust them.
The building sighs like a master at his novice.
We lie to ourselves that it's normal, this glow
of street light is better than the candles we'd
blow: their snuffed flames haunting like ghosts
of posterity, the lucent lives we left back home.

05/08/15// Diary Entry #18

This is how I found 1997's poem: by looking through the Poetry Book Society recommendations for the work of female poets. I drew up a shortlist of books by Fleur Adcock, Patricia Beer, Ruth Sharman, Mimi Khalvati, Jean 'Binta' Breeze, Lavinia Greenlaw, Anne Rouse, Ruth Fainlight, Gillian Ferguson and Helen Dunmore. The first poem to stand out within my guidelines was 'The Pilgrim Fathers' from *Looking Back* by Fleur Adcock (Oxford Poets). After the first reading, I reckoned I'd be able to come up with a title close to hers and write about a similar experience. Her poem is about winning a competition...

> I got a Gold Star from the *Pilgrim Fathers*,
> my first public poem, when I was nine.
> I think I had to read it out to the class;
> but not one grilled me about it, line by line

...and the freedom of writing without fear of literary criticism. I'd be able to write about hopes I had at roughly that age, of becoming a visual artist and drawing freely without any refinement. I remembered, in 1997, painting a pink watering can as an assignment from art class. I considered sub-titling my poem 'The Red Watering Can', and alluding to William Carlos William's iconic 'Red Wheelbarrow'. I set the poem aside and carried on searching.

Patricia Beer's book *Autumn* was, as the title suggests, about the time of year and I could not find the voice of my younger self echoed in the body of work. I enjoyed Gillian Ferguson's book but for much the same reason, had to set it down. Hers is a close meditation of the natural world and I had just moved to a city and wanted to climb and conquer everything more than meditate on it. Lavinia Greenlaw's book was gorgeous but had no suitable poem and of all the books, I found Mimi Khalvati's *Entries On Light* (Carcanet), to be the most halting, captivating and meditative...

I'm opening
   the door of shadows
on a page. In the doorway
   stands a poem

like a girl in a dress
   I see through her
to her feelings –

...but the book is one long sequence and its length is disqualifying. After two hours, I was left with Fleur Adcock's book, and Ruth Sharman's book *Birth of the Owl Butterflies*, where two poems stood out: 'My Good Coat' and 'Fury'. I decided to read reviews of both books and discovered Fleur was a New Zealander, thereby disqualifying her, leaving Ruth. Ruth, I discovered is British, but the reviews I found, published when the book came out, were overwhelmingly negative.

Penniless Press said that save a single poem on sexuality and cruelty, "The rest feel for the most part like exercises in poetry." The *PN Review's* opening criticism seems to be that Ruth is a female writing about "themes that we have come to recognise as characteristically female". *Litrefreviews* said "Disappointing. Small ideas tidily executed" and further down the entry, I found what appeared to be a response from Ruth herself which said:

I disagree, this poem is my life.
– R. Sharman.

***

This week, Sean O'Brien wrote an unfavourable review of Jack Underwood's *Happiness* for *The Guardian*, and the indefatigable poetry critic, Dave Coates, reviewed Sean's review. To be brief and frank, Dave thinks Sean was way outta line and deftly explains why he thinks this. Full disclosure, Jack Underwood is a friend and I have taught poetry with his poems in schools and theatres. The first time I read 'Happiness', the title poem from the book, I had so visceral a reaction, that for fear of crying in public, I got off the bus I was on, walked down a quiet deserted street and found a place to sit. Time passed, I don't recall how long. Dave is also an acquaintance and under my graphic artist hat, I designed the Saboteur Award for Poetry Review that Dave won this year.

Nothing Sean O'Brien wrote changed my mind about how I felt or continue to feel about Jack's work. Similarly none of the reviews of Ruth's book will change how the playfulness of the first poem grabbed me and drew me through the book. In England I am part of a minority ethnic group that is subject to prejudice and Marina Tsvetayeva wrote 'In this most Christian of worlds, all poets are Jews'. For these and countless other notions, which I am yet to dissect, I am always drawn to underdogs. It seems the world was pitted against Ruth, so I am drawn to her. If indeed Ruth wrote the response to that post, then it is heartbreaking that she felt the need to, and in that, I find an anger I will channel into my poem. There are no coincidences. 1997 was the first time I was called a nigger. The word was hurled from a passerby in my new school. Ruth's poem *Fury* begins:

> I'm going to bag up
> the man who yelled 'Bitch'
> from a passing car
>
> with uncles who say
> they don't lay down the law
> but do...

It is a perfect match for the project.

1997
Ruth Sharman

From the book *Birth of the Owl Butterflies*

FURY

I'm going to bag up
the man who yelled 'Bitch'
from a passing car

with uncles who say
they don't lay down the law
but do, friends who trade

in spiteful truths,
that specialist too special
to talk things through . . .

and I'm going to give
the bag a good shake
until each marble-head

I never had the chance
to answer back
knocks against the next

with a crystalline crack;
then I'll tip them out
on the kitchen floor

and send them tumbling
under the fridge,
to lie among the piles

of dust and broken pills
where silverfish
are looking for lunch.

FURY 1997
#*After* Ruth Sharman

I'm going to bag up
the boy who yelled 'Nigger'
from his speeding bike

with uncles who say
their boxing days are gone
but gnaw their rebuilt fists,

with aunties who buried
razor blades in the men
who held them down,

their friends who trade
chicken-claw, powdered tusks
and scorpions

with their viper-tooth-
necklaced other friends
who only call at dusk

and I'm going to shake
the bag until the jagged-
edged arrow-head

I never got to shoot,
each snub-nosed
rock I never catapulted,

the flint stones
I never sparked, the mace
of crushed belt buckles

I never swung,
the rusted knuckles
of ancient chains,

whip-tips, branding
irons and all the glass-
and-grass-weaved

weaponry I failed
to let taste blood,
knocks against the next

with a crystalline crack.
Then I'll crash them out
on the kitchen floor,

send them tumbling
toward my booted feet
and look for what's left

of the kid: whole chunks
of white meat, loose
teeth, shredded sinew

the soft marble
of both his eyes,
the clump of brain

matter that divides
and conquerers,
his flapping tongue

which I will kick still
like stupefied fish
then invite the neighbour's

rottweilers in
who always
are looking for lunch.

19/08/15// Diary Entry #19
Doodle - 1998

1998
Ken Smith
From the book *Wild Root*

BEFORE THE LISBON TRIBUNAL

They asked why I came here. I replied
to hear the rain falling in the street,
footsteps running into the wet dark.
To consume fish and more fish, drink tinto,
branco, verde, secco, make love, sleep late,
waking to the calls of ships on the Tagus.

And the arrival of what ships did I wait for?

I described the *Alfama* winding on itself,
a heap of washing lines and lemon trees,
sardine scales underfoot, children tumbling
down its alleys. In the cold empty cathedral
what I felt was *cold, empty*, a barn
built by the thugs of the Second Crusade.

What could I tell them of this?

I spoke of *Guincho*, its name that means scream
for the Atlantic wind rushing through, days
watching the slow shift in the quick sea
arriving in walls of water, the sea's change
and the light's change till the round bowl
of the earth's rim's lost and the light gone.

And where did I think such light went?

They were amused, patient. Those were early days,
I was not yet accused. At my second examination
they were seven, young, clever, soft spoken,
a clerk scratching, his tongue between his teeth.
There were no charges, the questions random:
could a ship of armed men be hidden in a fist?

Did I believe their mares sired by the West Wind?

Did cheese produce mites, bad meat blowflies,
did a closed box of old rags generate mice?
I was to help clear up certain allegations,
they as anxious as I, and so forth, to be done.
I have pen, ink, paper, candle, a writing desk
and this white room wherein to write my confessions.

BEFORE THE IMMIGRATION TRIBUNAL 1998
#After Ken Smith

They asked why we came here. We replied
to master the meticulous small talk of weather,
sharpen instincts of forming ordered queues,
consume bland food, buckets of foreign beer,
chant football slogans at quiet commuters
and await good news from northern Nigeria.

And the arrival of what news did we wait for?

We described *Plateau State* burning itself,
a spreading undercurrent of intolerance
from the steeple-like hills to the moon and
star-studded desert. In the hot, stifled places
of worship, what we felt was *hot, stifled,*
a construct by the thugs of the British Empire.

What could we tell of the time before this?

We spoke of old *Sokoto,* its name that screams
of harmattan winds blowing through afternoons,
watching its slow drift cloak the sun in gold-dust,
what enchanting mystery the sky would become,
and this was all we feared before the Empire's arrival,
the shuddering nights after and that gold light gone.

And where did we think our gold light went?

They were amused, patient. In those early days,
we hadn't yet been refused. At our next hearing
they were seven, older, hard talking sceptics,
a clerk squinting, a pen between his teeth.
Their minds were made, the questions random:
could a car of armed men crush a mustard seed?

Did we think their guns came on Afghan wings?

Is the Queen *Haram*? John the Baptist black?
What message could a burning cross send back?
We were to help clear up their confusion,
they as impatient as we were to be done.
We had our nightmares, the scars on our skin
and that white room in which to confess or convince.

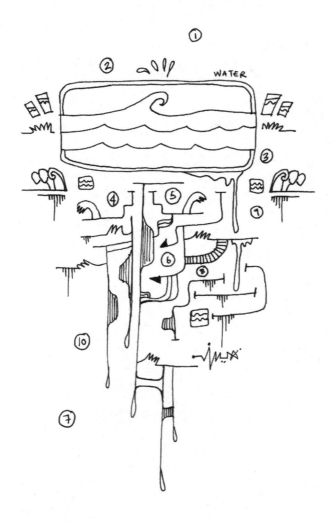

WATER

1999
Frieda Hughes

From the book *Wooroloo*

FIRE. 1.

It missed me twice.
The first time at the Candlestick stadium
It caught me in its black rain.
Its sky was sick with trees and gagged
By walls and wooden floors and small dogs,
Swallowed whole.

The second time,
I sat under my tin roof
And heard the ashes rattle in the gutter. Made a wish
With every one, like coins in water.
Its footsteps levelled oat fields and skinned trees,
Quick as locusts, hot as branding irons.

This time it shouted.
And I was out. Furious,
Its voice burst fat beneath tree bark
And the possums froze in their little ash-pose.
Brittle bones pinned black
In their burning hollow.

Still, I didn't hear.
It was louder now. The neighbour's sheep
Were cooked in a field corner, and the chickens blackened
Beyond possessing even a beak or claw to make them birds.
The garage buckled in pain,
Its window dripped from the window frame.

Fire called again.
I was too far away to see
My studio twitch with its disease.
It began with a small red spot
That flowered in the floorboards,
Its anemone danced, and the music
Was the crack of wood applauding.

I wasn't in the audience
When fire ate the metal roof like a rice cracker.
Left only crumbs, a dead fridge and bottles
That had mated in their molten passion,
Where once there was the corner of a room
Beneath a sink.

Fire was there when I returned,
Watching from smoke-stumps, and barely satisfied.
In bare, black fields rose twisted squares
That were sheds once. And the studio
Lay perfect on its plot, a fresh dug grave
Punctured only by its own ribcage.

But the house remained.
All the fire hoses had been and gone
And left it clean. Soot ran right up
To the verandah, where fire had stood calling
And not been heard. Even the water-tank
Was fresh.

Fire saw this.
Above the tank grew a vast tree, rotten with life
And crawling things. Fire had hollowed it out.
Still it burned. Fire drew itself together
For a final shout, and the tree exploded,
Left the tank tangled in limbs and emptying its broken cup.

Fire was still laughing
Three days later when, in the dark –
Like musical notes left over from a large opera –
The last flames echoed from their stumps.
Eyes unslept and lips curling,
Still eating.

And now I treat blackened saplings
With water drippers and a plastic tube,
As if the land were some mammoth animal
On life-support for a small cat.
And the last leaves of the tallest trees
Have this new death-voice
As their bloodless shells clatter.

WATER. 1. 1999
#After Frieda Hughes

It almost had me twice.
The first time at a leisure centre
in Maiduguri, one waterslide spat me
into a forest of legs, dense as swamp
-tree roots I slashed at, swallowing
till the lifeguard dived.

The second time,
attempting backflips in a surf, I felt
the wave draw back before I saw it
rise, claw-like, frothing at its mouth,
to fall and knock the compass out of
me till the shoreline dragged me back.

This time it waited.
At school, below the swim coach's
stern eyes, it never strayed outside
its narrow lanes or clawed at us kids
haplessly slapping its flat tongue.
It stayed silent, nonchalant.

Still, I didn't budge.
It lured me in like this: Samantha
was a fish in water Jack loved more
than our own after-school art club
so when he switched to swim club,
I joined to watch his romance burn.

But Water waited still.
I was too close to see the big picture:
Jack's deep scrutiny of Sam's breast
-stroke, that unconscious mimicry
of her front-crawl-form left him
a better swimmer, me far behind.

I wasn't in the audience
when he learnt the curious music
of underwater movement, to dance
its buoyancy between your legs,
to glide fillet-knife like, to work
human feet to functioning flippers.

Water was there when I returned,
watching from the shallows – curving
the long fluorescent lines of light into
thin humourless smiles – to the deep
where it turned storm-cloud dark,
and Jack cut through it all.

The pool remained quiet too
the Thursday afternoon we snuck in.
The swim teacher had been and gone.
The cleaners left the poolside dry,
the water still as mirrors, the deep just
as mysterious, Jack daring me to dive.

Water saw this.
When Jack dipped a toe and ripples
threw light whispering blue across
the pool's auditorium walls, moving
as I imagine spirits do, like melted
stars, and still I refused, Jack pushed.

Water was still laughing
minutes later when, like a fledgling
learning the clockwork of its wings,
I found that water's brand of flight
echoed out of me, from the deep to
the shallows, right back and beyond.

And now I treat poolsides
and shorelines, doorways, twilights,
sunshowers and shade – spaces where
our world is neither one thing or its
other – as sacred, earth's few places
to teach what surfaces or lies beneath,
what fights or flies inside us still.

16/ 09/15// Diary Entry #21

Last week, I was working in Paris where I finished the sixteenth poem of the project. Perhaps because of my close proximity to the refugee village in Calais, which is one of the focal points of the migration crisis and the various debates raging, including the use of the image of Alan Kurdi (the Syrian boy who drowned crossing the Mediterranean to Italy), as an immigrant, I felt even closer to the issue. So I did that arguably pointless act of venting my frustration by sharing an image that crossed my timeline –

– a deconstruction/response to the headline of an article by Melanie Phillips. I failed to track down whoever created the image and my tweet has since been shared 865 times and favourited 493. Now this is laughable, even insignificant by viral standards, but what it showed was a public interest in etymology and specifically in the language we used to 'other' people.

Halfway through searching for the seventeenth poem, I was interviewed by *Huck Magazine* and asked the question 'Why do you write?' and the answer I gave, the one I usually give, is to describe what it felt like to sit in Holland Park School, in my first class, and discover that the whole world was there. There were kids from Iran, Egypt, India, Bangladesh, Pakistan, Jamaica, Japan, Turkey, Algeria, France and Sweden all within touching distance. Before that, in Nigeria, every kid I'd schooled with was dark-skinned Nigerian. I thought these new kids looked as different to me as chalk is said to be from cheese, but the more time I spent with my new friends, the more I discovered not just very similar character traits and mannerisms but muscular movement beneath skin, small ripples and twitches that reminded me of friends in Nigeria. The profound effect this had on me, which it still has on me, is a belief that we are the same essential beings, that things like skin, race, pigmentation, language, accent, etc., are thin illusions we give weight to, or allow weight to be given to. I write to chip away at these illusions.

I think nations and borders are part of those illusions. I think they are nothing more than lines in the sand which the wind can shift, which the wind *does* shift, which is to say it is moved by something often gentle and invisible, which is to say myth, which is to say we are destroying each other for how the wind blows, which is to say the reasons are not good enough. I won't bother laying down the argument that Britain's colonial history, foreign policy and military escapades in the Middle East, Northern and Southern African countries are partially, if not the sole root cause of the crisis now... there seems to be collective amnesia or something. Also, this isn't the place for political historical discourse which requires or necessitates objective rigour. This is about poetry. However, selecting the poem for the year 2000 got me wondering if I had allowed the same illusion I write against to disqualify various poets.

The Poetry Book Society selections and recommendations for 2000 included books by Michael Donaghy, Maurice Riordan, August Kleinzahler, Matthew Sweeney, Alan Jenkins, Douglas Dunn, Michael Longley and George Szirtes. The project is to respond to poems by British poets, so I removed August from the list as he is American and lives there. Michael Donaghy is American but he settled, lived and died in London. Sweeney and Riordan are both Irish poets: Sweeney used to live here and Riordan is the current editor of *Poetry Review*, and lives in my corner of the world: South London. They have contributed more to British Poetry than I have, immigrants all, as I am, and I can't bring myself to disqualify them on nation-basis. Michael's contains the unforgettable poem 'Black Ice and Rain' and I adored 'Make Believe' by Maurice Riordan, but the poem I choose called 'A European Dream' is by Douglas Dunn, who fortunately is a Scotsman.

'A European Dream' is a dense, sensual, exhilarating whirlwind journey through Europe through Poland, Sweden, France, Lithuania, going back and forth in time, full of history, music, forests, swords, crankshafts and armour; about what may or may not have happened. My family and I moved to Dublin in 1999 and I want to write about a phone call I had from Jack (who taught me how to swim in the previous poem) in 2000 – updating me on all that I had missed out on – and the word 'Sonder'. On Youtube, you can find a video that explains its meaning exquisitely, and this definition taken from *The Dictionary of Obscure Sorrows** is also illustrative:

> **Sonder:**
> n. the realization that each random passerby is living a life as vivid and complex as your own – populated with their own ambitions, friends, routines, worries and inherited craziness – an epic story that continues invisibly around you like an anthill sprawling deep underground, with elaborate passageways to thousands of other lives that you'll never know existed, in which you might appear only once, as an extra sipping coffee in the background, as a blur of traffic passing on the highway, as a lighted window at dusk.

Next week I start writing, chipping away at the illusion yet again, and as always.

* see: www.dictionaryofobscuresorrows.com

2000
Douglas Dunn

From the book *The Year's Afternoon*

A EUROPEAN DREAM

I dreamt I missed the bus from Łomza down to Warsaw.
It was raining, a rain that varnished skin and clothes.
I wandered past the turn for Ostrałenka, preferring
Views of thin horses in pastures by stagnant roadsides
To thumbable cars and big trucks from Gdynia and Gdansk.
Policemen, farmers, and postmen with airmails passed me;
They paid me no attention, in my thornproof Border tweeds
My briefcase and umbrella, as my Scottish brogues
Leathered the tarmac, a credit to Hoggs of Fife.
They might have thought me just another journalist
Pedestrian factfinding in industrial Ruritania
Instead of someone dreaming what almost happened.
Words in my mouth, as I talked to myself, were strangers
To each other. Cross roads' traffic, changing gear in Polish,
Was language of great charm and great Copernicus,
Spoken Chopin, the passion of Slavonic eloquence.
Night fell with cushioned landings on the active forests.
Wooded nocturnes made me feel that the continent
Widened across humanity's north-European plain
As tops of conifers twinkled in the starlight
With epic whisperings that said 'Pan Tadeusz, Pan Tadeusz'.
Wolf, bear and bison staggered from the dens of species,
Hunted down, parked, tamed, zoo'd, or modernized,
Turned into jerkins or the privileged plateful.
Time, too, was walking in the night, counting the graves,
Re-paragraphing chronicles of howls and tears.
I heard a river wash its scraps of sunken armour.
Sword-shards, helmets, crankshafts, to a listening ear

112

Sounded as sub-aqueous and subterranean nudges
On skulls and bones and residue of hoof and steel,
Eyes and flesh, the pure substance of massed memories, melted
Into historical compost. I dreamt the darkest night
I ever knew and time was strolling beside me
Down that road at the hour of no cars and no one. Time
Felt disinclined to lend a hand and help me through.
'Feel hard and think historical' – I left the road
Out of obedience to my sturdy aphorism
With golf umbrella up and a firmly gripped briefcase
And through long, lighted windows I saw kissing of hands
At a big do beneath archaic chandeliers
As chauffeurs polished limousines by candlelight,
Their little vodkas balanced on their polished cars.
For several surreal moments I was at the soirée
Kissing the hand of this one, that one, being diplomatic,
Temporarily suave in black tie and dinner jacket
Or just as out-of-place in Border tweed (three piece)
Among the ball-gowned and Old European tuxedo'd
Counts and Margraves, leaders, luminaries, a cardinal,
A consumptive poet, generals, celebrated courtesans,
Which is to say too little of East Prussians,
Muscovian footpads, Lithuanians and leather Scots
Pedlars and mercenaries, Swedes, Red Cavalrymen,
Ubiquitous Italian waiters and Parisian chefs
Voluble with genius and pedigree'd certification,
Greatcoated Tartar grooms and Cossack major-domos.
Then I was fighting off the tugs and rips of briars
In multiplying forests, or watching my wife
Led one way and my children the other, myself that way,
At the dummy station among the tight-leashed dogs
In the stench of cattle-truck excrement, with glimpsed timetables
Listing departures for Vienna, and *that* city, and *that* town,
And the grin of the officer with his hands on his hips.
Bon voyage! I shouted, as I ran through the forest

In the endless night, very deep with timber inwit,
Running like a tormented innocent through slumber
Twisted by European odiousness and what happened
In that neck of the woods. *Bon voyage!* I cried again
To myself and the millions as I ran on,
Umbrella ripped from my hand and my briefcase dropped
Into a gurgling drainage ditch, my 'life's work '
Bundled down to its watery rot where croaking toads live
And my suit made by Stewart and Christie of Edinburgh
Ripped into the rags of one hungering for want, torn by
Hunger for hunger and a loud curse on all comfort,
Hunger for lyrical anger, for righteous indignation,
Vituperative and lonely in the forests of hopelessness
I woke up as a man beaten, scratched and filthy
In the torn clothes of an interior adventure
Shouting, 'Shrive me more for what I haven't committed!
Negate even my soul if I have one as I plead before
The pagan God of Kindness who doesn't exist!'
History's wide boys and murderers tittered and giggled,
Experts in *mauvaise foi,* forgetfulness, and shameless
Persistence in their arts of perpetuity and success.
'Goodbye,' I said to myself, parting company with
My own certainties, my body, my name, my language.
It is disagreeable, to tend your garden, on your knees,
With the sensation of tending millions of graves.

AN ENGLISH DREAM 2000
#*After* **Douglas Dunn**

I dreamt I missed the bus from Firhouse to Temple Bar.
When rain cut through the dense tree I sheltered under,
I wandered out down the turn for Ballycullen, preferring
views of drenched mattresses by footpaths in patchy fields
to family cars and cyclists from Friarstown and Kiltipper.
Gardeners, travellers, postmen and priests passed me;
they frowned, all turning to stare at my low-slung jeans,
backpack and t-shirt soaked to my skin and my trainers
squelching the cracked tarmac loudly through the rain.
They might have thought me another fragile immigrant
desperate for help, knocking from door to stranger's door,
instead of someone dreaming of what might've happened
if Jack hadn't called. I talked to myself: of that upper deck
of the bus where I had sat, my head pressed to the window,
of the rain's throbbing drops, each like a bulb of thought
exploding against the glass – like an invisible force-field
or bubble only I floated in – when Jack's call shattered it
and whatever it is I was inside felt like a small continent
widening out from humanity's west-European plains to
west-African valleys, to the backyards of my childhood
and there, friends whispering 'bet he won't remember us'.
I remembered, but had frozen them in memory – Jack at
the last time we hung out after school, at Notting Hill when
he waved bye from the bus stop, a sepia sun framing him.
Time began melting as he spoke, pulling, from the graves
of old conversations, new strands of talk – how Priya had
married the man from Bangladesh; it had been arranged
since birth. How Macey finally stopped calling her a bitch
the Tuesday afternoon news broke, how they had become
best friends till Priya's flight took off. How Mitchell was

expelled for slugging Mr Luger – the hard nut of his fist
dripping teacher-blood. How Marcel's lungs had grown
as his waist band to dominate whenever choir rehearsed.
How Jack had become a rung in choir's ladder and every
rung wished for Marcel's fall. How the much-speculated-
on mythic architecture of Eugenia's bra was a wonder no
longer, a myth no more, for John stole it one swim class
and sliced back its fabric revealing underwire, and the boys
praised his pursuit of knowledge and above the interlocking
of our student lives, our dubious teachers still loomed large;
how Mr Thom Erinton who still mourned his teenage rock
-band, now strummed lunchtimes away in his office and
goth kids gathered to loiter his doorway, finding kinship
in the solemn of his strings. How when Cameron nicked
the headmistress's bottle, what burned his throat was cold
and clear vodka. How Mr Summercorn's son who schooled
among us brought his father's madness down to the fields,
had dragged Mr Summercorn's drama practice out to make
theatre of football games, and the threatening war finally
broke between Moroccan and Caribbean kids… All this Jack
spoke, marching their stories down the phone-line, feeding
me, and leading the march, small stories of him: what had
passed in his life since I'd left it, what small loves he'd lost,
what smaller ones he'd won, how the questioning of where
on Earth I'd gone passed from annoying till no one asked.
Then I was fighting for my crumbling world and watching
in multiplying fractures the bubble of it burst, the cracks
leading one way, holes down the other and myself peering
from inside its falling walls, out, at who crowded the bus:
at the blue coat across and the woman inside, at the backpack beside and whose back it hugged, at the golden wrist
watch and who watched the wrist. I watched on as the bus
surfed a hill and Dublin's City centre lay sprawled beneath
in the endless thousands of pedestrians. And I joined them,

running like a tormented child through whispering trees
asking of the blazer and her rolled-up sleeves, of the silver
necktie and his stetson's brim, of the walking stick and who
walked with, of the tight-fisted child, its tight-lipped mother
of her tight-gripped cigarette, of that cigarette butt, of who
managed the factory where it came from, of who scrubbed
the factory's tobacco-tanned floor and who rubbed her feet
when the work was done... if all of them had loved and lost
as Jack did, if they too had as interlocking worlds, if theirs
were nuanced as mine was; And if they were protagonists
in the novel of their lives, if I was a side character? Or less
than a paragraph? How short a line, or flicker in a dream?
I woke up as an older boy battered, scared and faithless in
the torn clothes of an interior adventure, its loose thread
spooling like chains around my feet and what was set free
afraid to test its wings. And years later I'd learn the word
'Sonder' – *n.* the obscure sorrow of acknowledging we sit
in the peripheries of most of whom we see: at best we are
passing ships, faint ripples, drips, at worst insignificant to
no thing at all – all this I'd have missed if he hadn't called.
'Goodbye,' I said to who I once was, parting company with
my own certainties, the world I inhabited before Jack's call,
it's thin narrative, freestyled plot, its structure now soaked
with the sensation of discovering millions of lives
and the selfish wish I get to live mine long.

14/ 10/15// Diary Entry #22

Today I began looking for the eighteenth poem, but last Saturday I gave a talk at TEDx Brixton about the changing nature of masculinity, about barber shops and about depression in men. It was built around a research trip for a play, an incident with my three-year-old nephew Malachi, and the subject matter I want to deal with in this poem: in my penultimate year in Dublin, in 2001, a close friend of mine called Steven took his own life.

It profoundly changed the way I thought about everything; knowledge, trust, emotion, truth, meaning, language, poetry, freedom and friendship. Steven loved talking and our relationship thrived on argument. It was the bridge on which we met during my early days in Ireland. There, racism and ignorance was so thriving that my sister was once asked by a random passenger on a bus if she got her period like 'normal' people. In the midst of it all, Steven and I discovered a mutual respect and love for language in each other and our time for bantering became crystals, jewels we guarded during those mundane school lessons; trying to outdo each other, purely for the sake of using words dazzlingly. He used to call me Shake-Ell-Speare or SheikEllmspeare – a nod to my Muslim/North African cultural heritage and to William Shakespeare. Steven thought I'd be a writer long before I ever considered it and I started writing the late summer after he was buried. I wanted to fill up the time we'd usually spend arguing or making each other laugh in school, with something... anything. I tried to recreate our arguments, to invent some new ones, to trap them in verse, which eventually, unavoidably led to mimicking Shakespeare's voice. I was terrible at it.

In Steven's final hours, he called or texted everyone in our small group of friends. Days after, we pieced together everything and saw that all his messages added up to a final wave, that he was saying goodbye to us, individually. We did not understand or see this as it happened. The only person Steven didn't call or text was me. It haunted me for years. It still does. I questioned if I had been a good enough friend. If I had offended him in the days before somehow. If he just didn't think it was worth dropping me a line. If his phone ran out of battery. I went wild with reasons and reasoning. It haunts me still.

Out on a date a few years ago, I spoke about this to the lady I was with who suggested something I never considered: perhaps Steven didn't contact me because he knew I was the only person who could talk him out of it. I ran away from the table, into the men's toilet, stayed and stood there for eleven full minutes until my breath became regular and blood returned to my face. I don't know what to think and still have not deconstructed what that means or might have meant. I have been avoiding writing about this for fourteen years, but I think I can do this now.

The task then is to find a poem on this subject matter or one broad enough that I can write a response to about Steven. I start by looking through *The Poetry Review* and the Poetry Book Society Recommendations for 2001 and I find poems by Lavinia Greenlaw, Helen Dunmore, Colette Bryce and Elizabeth Bartlett. 'The Spirit Staircase', 'The Man on the Roof', 'The Word' and 'The Burden' are their poem-titles respectively and some are just so close to how Steven took his life, that I shake and shrink from them. They are gorgeous poems and 'The Word' by Colette Bryce, which is about Jesus Christ and what was done to him, is broad enough. I put this to one side.

Of the Poetry Book Society recommendations, I look through Gillian Allnutt's *Lintel*, Wendy Cope's *If I Don't Know*, Tracey Herd's *Dead Redhead*, Selima Hill's *Bunny*, Pascale Petit's *The Zoo Father* and Helen Dunmore's *Out of the Blue*. They are fantastic as they are haunting. *Bunny* is melancholic and beautiful, *Dead Redhead* is astoundingly inventive, *Out of the Blue* is lyrically stupefying but *The Zoo Father* took my breath away over and over again. I read it a few years ago when the poet Jay Bernard, to prove one could write magical-realist, yet physical and visceral poetry, simply gave me a poem from book to read and walked away without staying to find out if she'd convinced me. She had. Re-reading Pascale Petit's book again, with this new intention, feels like having a late low-lit lunch with an old weathered friend and finding painful truths anew.

At the day's end, I am left with these poems to choose from:
'My Father's Lungs' – Pascale Petit
'The Word' – Colette Bryce
'If Only' – Helen Dunmore.

Though I am terrified of where this will take me emotionally, down memory lane or beyond, I'll begin writing later tonight.

2001
Pascale Petit
From the book *The Zoo Father*

MY FATHER'S LUNGS

All day I have been shrinking
and my father has been turning transparent.
There were moments when I held his soul
in a little tuft of eagle down,
while his dressing-gown and pyjamas
glowed like clothes of light.
We've drunk two bottles of champagne.
I've begun to see the entire
fauna of a forest in him.
It's like looking at a glass frog –
I can see through his clear blue skin
into his heart. But I'm no longer interested
in whether he loves me or not,
or if he really thought of me
every day of his years away.
I'm looking at those luminous trees
growing in his rib cage,
to replace his choked lungs.
I'm piercing his body membrane,
I'm so small now, it's like the skin of a sky
I can fly through, into his chest.
His breath is amplified all around me.
His lungs are white, shining
like X-rays in this twilight.
They branch in all directions
in a left and right garden,
separated by a stream.
His breath is separating into four winds –

the white, black, red and blue
that make coloured sounds, and sometimes
an octave of pure silver
as I watch an upper branch
burst into a swirl of starlight.
The grass is red, and wafts my feet
towards my next task:
I am gathering lungmoss for my pillow,
making a bed in his body.

STEVEN'S LUNGS 2001
#*After* Pascale Petit

All day I have been shaking
and Steven has been growing cold.
There were moments before when he held my gaze
in fits of soaring laughter
while houses, whole ghost towns of lonely
glowed heavy in him.
We've walked past his coffin twice.
I've begun to see the entire
network of a hollow city in his chest.
It's like looking at a scorched brooch –
I can see through his dark suit
into his heart. But I don't want to know
when or where he learnt to loop a noose
or how, I want to ask why he called
everyone but me to say goodbye.
I'm looking at the radio transmitters
growing in his rib cage
to replace his still lungs.
I'm piercing his white noise.
I'm so small now, it's like his skin is static
I can fall through, into his chest.
His breath is the quiet that echoes back.
His lungs are dust-grey and glinting
like metallic trees in the twilight.
They branch in all directions,
in two constructs of twisted iron
separated by a thin path.
His innermost thoughts litter the road –
the green, blue and brown scraps of wire
that aren't connected, but sometimes

an old pulse will ghost through
as I watch; a handful will
burst into a thin scratch of consonants.
The ground amplifies, and draws my hands
towards my next task:
I am gathering them into an answer,
making an altar, resurrecting his voice.

28/10/15// Diary Entry #23

Today I began writing the nineteenth and final poem of the *#Afterhours* project. Years ago, during a mini-nervous breakdown, the writer and musician Musa Okwonga sat down with me and in one of the most devastating and rewarding conversations I've ever had, told me that everything I write comes down to three words: Identity, Displacement and Destiny – that they are the square roots, the common denominators, the grounds on which my everything stands. That night I looked at all I'd written and found that Musa couldn't have been more accurate.

'Identity' is there; my Irish/English/Nigerian-hood is the Rubik's Cube I keep unpacking, the gift that keeps giving. 'Displacement' is very much intertwined with this: finding myself in new countries led to attempts to fit in, which led to issues of identity. Displacement and the effects of moving, of being moved, of attempting to stay still, still taints all aspects of my life. 'Destiny' however is the most elusive, the 'holy spirit' of the trinity, of Musa's theory, and it is no wonder, as it is largely about faith, belief.

I was born to a Muslim father and a Christian mother and, whereas my sisters only ever went to Churches, I accompanied my father to Mosques, dressed exactly as a smaller version of him, thus from an early age, I had a plurality of religious belief. My father converted to Christianity eventually, as I did, but those early memories stayed with me and arriving in London, learning about other religions in school, I found that their commonalities settled in me, far outweighing their differences. What religion conjures in me now is a kind of spirituality, a kind of faith, a belief in a vague order to things, and that I will find that order if I look for it; a path will always emerge.

I'd say faith pilots every immigrant journey, and blind faith at that. Hope is there, eternally, ubiquitously, but that f-word sharpens hope into a weapon. It gives hope form. Faith points hope towards a destination, towards a promised and an un-promised land, through deserts, jungles, oceans – it is that vast and unquenchable.

I think poetry is impossible without faith. When you begin writing and are unsure about what is happening on the page, what powers the pen is faith that meaning will be made, that a vague reason and order will rise from the impulse to write. This is faith working towards the poem's destination and every poem has its destiny. The reading of poetry also requires faith and when we find a poem satisfactory, it is the vindication of our faith – proof that we were right all along to allow the poem to enter us.

Whenever I am too focused on the destination of a poem or play and I begin to question the faith that is powering me, thinking myself too arrogant in my belief, I look for signs that I am on the right path. This *#Afterhours* project has been riddled with signs right from the start, right from the get-go, too numerous to write about. Here, I'll just focus on signs surrounding this last poem.

1/ I began this project to mark the end of childhood, to mark turning 30. I turned 31 last Friday and this first week of being 31, I am in Nigeria for the first ever Lagos International Poetry Festival. There is a circularity here, a sort of – prodigal son returning home after he has become a man to finish off writing about his childhood type of circularity. I am also researching, coincidentally, a play for the Royal Shakespeare Company and the play is an attempt to write a prequel to Shakespeare's *The Tempest* from Caliban's point of view, echoing my first attempts at poetry which were imitations of Shakespeare.

2/ After moving to Dublin, I returned to London in 2002 and began poking around poetry. At the time, Andrew Motion was

Poet Laureate and his first book under that laureateship was published in 2002. This project could be framed as an attempt to add a voice of the colonised to the shelves of the colonisers, by writing response-poems to those in the British cannon. In that light it is fitting to end *#Afterhours* in response to the Poet Laureate at the time.

3/ This book of Andrew's, *Public Property*, begins with a long sequence. The third poem of that sequence is, incredibly enough, called 'The Aftermath', perfect one might say with which to end a project called *#Afterhours*. The poem is about a return to childhood (!) specifically, about trying to return to the memory of a place (Welsh word! Hiraeth!), or an actual place visited decades before, as I have been trying to do throughout this project, and contains the incredibly poignant, perfect lines:

> The thing I could not see, stumbling through the trees,
> across the ditch, and then the stubble-spread, was how
>
> it would still be going on years later, still going on now,
> in the long aftermath since I have tried to reach there again,

The thing I could not see when I started this project last October, was how writing about childhood would be governed by the search for home, that Musa's themes of Identity, Displacement and Destiny began way before I was born, in the lives of my grandparents and in my parents; that it would still be going on years later, and still going on now. My earliest memory of returning to London in 2002 is packing my bag with food one evening and going for a long directionless walk, an attempt to get lost in the city of London and see what was out there. This eventually became The Midnight Run, a project I founded in 2005. The Midnight Run is a walking, arts-filled, night-time cultural journey through urban spaces that gathers strangers and local artists/activists to explore, play and create whilst the city sleeps. There have been Midnight Runs in London,

Manchester, Paris, Berlin, Rome, Florence, Madrid, Barcelona, Auckland, Perth and many, many more across England. It is an endeavour that both challenges and confirms my humanity each time. Back in 2002 though, all I wanted to do was get lost. This is exactly what Andrew does in his poem, he loses himself in the woods and fields around his home. It is impossible to read Andrew's poem without a faith in its destination, in its destiny; it is long, narrative, detailed, full of youthful spirit and of the kind of spirituality one feels among nature. I will attempt to keep this alive in my version, an 'urban spirituality' if you will, instead of nature's spirituality. Urban Spirituality, which is a concept I have been poking at for the last year or so, will become the focus of future writing. In a sense then, this last poem, as much as it is an end, is a beginning.

To me, these are signs I am on a right path, that *#Afterhours* was somehow destined and I am at its end, its clear destiny. Or perhaps I'm reading waaaay too much into this, should chill the fuck out and write the damn poem, which I will now. It is morning here in Nigeria. The sun is proving its dominance of the city, the heat pouring down. I have just returned from an early morning radio show publicising the poetry festival, returned to my desk, to this poem. Andrew begins...

I am a child again, going walkabout by day

I'll begin...

I feel like an exiled child, going walkabout by night.

2002
Andrew Motion
From the book *Public Property*

from 'A Long Story'
3. THE AFTERMATH

I am a child again, going walkabout by day
for the first time, packing everything I can imagine
to take with me: one cheese sandwich, one tomato,
one Cox's apple, one pack of cards, and one torch.

It is not much, but it is enough. I shall never come
back and I shall drink from a stream. In fact I am
thirsty already, and only half way over the village
green, where the butcher sees me, Mr Wilkinson,

lifting one red arm in his doorway; I can just
make out his blue-striped apron, and imagine
the sawdust with its patterns of coming and going.
He doesn't know I'm off for ever. He thinks

I'm carrying a bag with fruit and bread
for Mrs Reynolds, whose husband died.
Sunlight bores from the hard centre of the sky,
and the butcher melts under his awning –

he is the last thing I see before the main road,
which in those days was not main, and soon
dropped behind me with a meagre lorry-rumble
and quick car-fizz, when what I'd hoped for

was the stupendously huge thunderous passing
of a combine, the tarmac wrinkled by sheer weight,
and a queue of drivers behind wanting to feel angry
but in truth children like me, entertained and patient.

It was that time of year, the aftermath, and when
I scraped over a barred gate on the far side of the road
a field they had already cut was lying entirely open.
I had never been there before, and had never felt

such emptiness under a wide heaven. With hedges
grubbed out, and close-cropped stubble swelling
and sinking for such a blinding distance, and sky
lifted yet at the same time crushing onto me

– with all this, my head was travelling
at ground level, hunting for a sense of balance.
Did I keep moving forward? I did, at a snail's pace,
hauling myself up the speckled crest of a dock-leaf,

then roller-coasting into a rubble of dry earth-crumbs,
ant eggs and wheat husks. Everything was fascinating
but an obstacle, and I had to examine the least detail:
a straw stem, a flint scale, a wormcast like wet ribbon.

How did I miss the spinney, moored there in mid-field?
By keeping my head down, as I say. By not looking
at the larger thing, or what was happening. But these
were real and solid trees which squeezed round me:

satin-skinned beeches; disgruntled oaks;
and a birch with leaves like grease spots.
Everything was as it should be, yet the dead twigs
went so quiet underfoot I might have been on air –

and it was cold, too, though the sun still danced
round the spinney on all sides, sticking in thin pins
and knife-blades, trying to get at me and failing.
I found a fallen tree near the centre, a young ash

with its leaf-hair mussed and threadbare, its root-ball
like a stubbed-out cigarette, and straight away
sat down, dizzy in the fug of mushroom-rot.
A collar dove landed in a flurry, then came back

under control with a display of wing-origami;
a bright orange spider abseiled from the root-stub;
the sun-blades kept up their dare-devil lancing
but missed me by so much, I might not have existed.

I had never planned it, but I felt myself dissolving –
my heart slowing to nothing, my brain running out,
all of me adrift in a mote-dance of dust and spores
and happy, until the sunlight sheathed its blades,

the spinney cooled and blackened, and the duller
silence told me I was hungry and expected home.
The thing I could not see, stumbling through the trees,
across the ditch, and then the stubble-spread, was how

it would still be going on years later, still going on now,
in the long aftermath since I have tried to reach there again,
setting off in secret across the hot village green
with the butcher lifting his red arm, the plastic bag

cumbersome and sticky in my hand, the traffic quiet,
and the enormous field opening before me, in which
there was never a single tree, much less a spinney,
but the whole expanse just clear and flat for ever.

THE AFTERMATH 2002
Part 3, from A Long Story
#*After* Andrew Motion

I feel like an exiled child going walkabout by night
for the first time, packing everything I can imagine
I'll need: spare socks, rain coat, assorted fruit, map
of central London, notebooks, pencils and a torch.

It's not much, but it's enough to loose myself with,
exploring the hard labyrinth of the city. In fact I am
already lost, and only half an hour out the block
of flats, when the landlady sees me, Mrs Adeyemi,

dragging a trolley of yams and plantains; I can just
make out her faded ankara head wrap, and imagine
its pattern of fleeing falcons frozen as I am, mid flight.
She doesn't know I'm off to find new space. She thinks

my backpack is stacked with biographies, novels
and films from the library which are long overdue.
The soft blanket of dusk is falling from the sky
and the landlady is vanishing into its darkness –

she is the last thing I see before the main road,
which is excessively proving its name, deafening
with the stupendously huge thunderous passing
of fire trucks and sirens, when all I'd prepared for

was the plodding procession of rush hour traffic,
meagre fish-tailing cyclists clicking by and trickles
of head-phoned-pedestrians wanting to be moved
by another beat but in truth, like me, tied to the city.

It was that time of year, the aftermath, and when
I ducked under a barrier on the far side of the road,
a monstrous building site was lying entirely desolate.
I had never been there before, and had never felt

such vast enclosed emptiness. With greasy puddles
and a solitary steel-rod rammed into a square
pool of cement, pointing upwards at the sky,
which at the same time was filtering light onto me

– with all this, my head was travelling
at ground level, hunting for a sense of balance.
Did I keep moving forward? I did, at a mouse's pace,
tumbling through a speckled nest of cigarette stubs,

then squeezing past a broken chainmail of crushed
beer cans and crown caps. Everything was an obstacle
but fascinating, and I had to list down the least detail:
a belt buckle, a razor, used condom like a flattened slug.

How did I miss the old multi-storey carpark mid-centre?
By keeping my head down, as I say, by not looking
at larger things, or what was happening. But there
were real and solid sign posts which announced:

bursting dustbins, proud bollards, parking spaces
– their grey lines like tired arms open to embrace cars.
Everything was as it should be, yet the newspapers
crunched so quiet underfoot I might have been on air –

and it was warm, too, though the moon still danced
round the carpark on all sides, throwing in broad beams
and sword-blades of light at me, hitting home each time.
I found neon signage near the centre, a poor thing

with its wires burnt and hanging out, its black paint
like a shedding second skin, and straight away
sat down, dizzy in the fug of asbestos-dust.
Two pigeons took off in a flurry, then came back

with a synchronised display of ballroom quickstep,
a Rorschach test of a moth fluttered from shadows;
the moon-blades kept up their ninja-like lancing
and struck me so often, I might have bled to death.

I had never planned it, but I felt myself solidifying –
my heart racing to fullness, my brain expanding out,
all of me alive in a mote-dance of dust and soot
and happy, until the moonlight sheathed its blades,

the carpark warmed and brightened, and the sharper
noises made a rhythm that merged with my own beat.
The thing I could not see, stumbling past street lights,
across traffic islands and then the main road, was how

it'd still be going on for years to come, still go on now.
In the long aftermath since, I've tried to reach there again,
setting off in secret across the cold urban courtyard
with the landlady lifting her head wrap, the backpack

packed well and sturdy in my hands, the traffic noisy,
and the vast building site opening before me, in which
I don't find a single street lamp, much less a carpark,
but the whole enclosure empty, and flat for ever.

28/10/15// Diary Entry #24

If the project were to continue, the poem I'd write for 2003, when I turned 19, would involve a little pornography, for that is how I found a poetry community in London. One June night, watching an adult television programme, HBO's *Real Sex* on Channel 5, I saw a woman reading a poem on a stage as another, completely nude, danced erotically to its rhythm. I lunged for the computer, Google-searched 'Poetry London' and the first event I found was called 'Aroma Poetry'. I went along and there, met its host and organiser, Nii Ayikwei Parkes. When I finally plucked up the courage to share one of the things I'd scribbled during my 'Aftermath'-like dérives through the city, Nii told me he liked it and asked me to return.

I have no doubt whatsoever that whatever it was I read was horrendous, but that act of acknowledgement (and perhaps kindness) from Nii changed my whole life. He'd go on to suggest poets to read, events to visit and he welcome me into his poetry family, many of whom remain friends and unofficial mentors. They embraced the wondering, questioning, lost young man I was and showed him another way of being. Lebo Mashile, the South African poet, says "The work of being an artist is intimately linked with the work of personal development"... and for all the deep catharsis of this project, for the opportunity it has given to excavate and reset unsettling aspects of those years, that work of personal development continues.

#Afterhours Reading List

Fleur Adcock – *Looking Back* (Oxford Poets, 1997)

Gillian Allnutt – *Lintel* (Bloodaxe Books, 2001)

Moniza Alvi – *The Country at My Shoulder* (Oxford Poets, 1997)

Simon Armitage – *Kid* (Faber and Faber, 1992 / 2002)

Simon Armitage – *Zoom* (Bloodaxe Books, 1989)

John Ash – *Disbelief* (Carcanet Press, 1987)

Elizabeth Bartlett – *Appetites of Love* (Bloodaxe Books, 2001)

Patricia Beer – *Autumn* (Carcanet Press, 1997)

Jay Bernard – *The Red and Yellow Nothing* (Ink, Sweat & Tears
    Press, 2016)

Jean 'Binta' Breeze – *On the Edge of an Island* (Bloodaxe Books, 1997)

Basil Bunting – *Briggflatts (Bloodaxe Books, 2009)*

John Burnside – *The Light Trap* (Cape Poetry, 2002)

Kayo Chingonyi – *Some Bright Elegance* (Salt Publishing, 2012)

Wendy Cope – *If I Don't Know* (Faber and Faber, 2001)

Robert Crawford – *A Scottish Assembly* (Chatto & Windus, 1990)

Ian Crichton Smith – *The Exiles* (Carcanet Press Limited, 1984)

Fred D'Aguiar – *Bill of Rights* (Chatto & Windus, 1998)

Michael Donaghy – *Conjure (Picador, 2000)*

Carol Ann Duffy – *Standing Female Nude (Picador, 2016)*

Ian Duhig – *Nominies* (Bloodaxe Books, 1998)

Helen Dunmore – *Bestiary* (Bloodaxe Books, 1997)

Helen Dunmore – *Out of the Blue: Poems 1975-2001*
    (Bloodaxe Books, 2001)

Helen Dunmore – *Short Days, Long Nights: New and Selected Poems*
    (Bloodaxe Books, 1991)

Douglas Dunn – *The Year's Afternoon* (Faber and Faber, 2000).

Paul Durcan – *Life Is A Dream: 40 Years Reading Poems, 1967 - 2007*
(Harvill Secker, 2009)

Ruth Fainlight – *Sugar Paper Blue* (Bloodaxe Books, 1997)

Gillian Ferguson – *Air for sleeping fish* (Bloodaxe Books, 1997)

Lavinia Greenlaw – *A World Where News Travelled Slowly* (Faber and Faber, 2016)

Bill Griffiths – *A Tract Against The Giants* (Coach House Press, 1984)

Phillip Gross – *Cat's Whisker* (Faber and Faber, 1987)

David Harsent – *Mister Punch* (Oxford Poets, 1984)

Tony Harrison – *V* (Bloodaxe Books, 1989)

Seamus Heaney – *The Haw Lantern* (Faber and Faber, 1987)

W.N. Herbert – *Cabaret McGonagall* (Bloodaxe Books, 1996)

Tracey Herd – *Dead Redhead* (Bloodaxe Books, 2001)

Geoffrey Hill – *The Orchards of Syon* (Penguin Books, 2002)

Selima Hill – *Bunny* (Bloodaxe Books, 2001)

Michael Hofmann – *Acrimony* (Faber and Faber Limited, 1986)

Frieda Hughes – *Wooroloo* (Bloodaxe Books, 1999)

Alan Jenkins – *The Drift* (Chatto & Windus, 2000)

Michael Jordan – *Space Jam* (Warner Home Video, 2001)

Jackie Kay – *Adoption Papers* (Bloodaxe Books, 1998)

Mimi Khalvati – *Entries on Light* (Carcanet Press, 1997)

August Kleinzahler – *Live from the Hong Kong Nile Club* (Faber and Faber, 2000)

Tom Leonard – *Intimate Voices: Selected Works, 1965-83* (Galloping Dog Press, 1984)

Michael Longley – *The Weather in Japan* (Wake Forest University Press, 2000)

Audre Lourde – *Zami: A New Spelling of My Name* (Crossing Press, 2001)

Sarah Maguire – *Spilt Milk* (Secker and Warburg, 1991)

Glyn Maxwell – *The Breakage* (Faber and Faber, 1998)

Blake Morrison – *Dark Glasses* (Chatto & Windus, 1989)

Andrew Motion – *Public Property* (Faber and Faber, 2003)

Paul Muldoon – *Meeting the British* (Faber and Faber, 1987)

Miriam Nash – *Small Change* (Flipped Eye Publishing, 2013)

Ben Okri – *The Famished Road* (Vintage Classics, 1992)

Tom Paulin – *The Invasion Handbook* (Faber and Faber, 2003)

Pascale Petit – *The Zoo Father* (Seren, 2001).

Terry Pratchett – *Pyramids* (Corgi, 1989 / 2012)

Craig Raine – *Rich* (Faber and Faber, 1984)

Peter Reading – *Faunal* (Bloodaxe Books, 2002)

Peter Redgrove – *In the Hall of the Saurians* (Secker & Warburg 1987)

Maurice Riordan – *Floods* (Faber and Faber, 2000)

Robin Robertson – *Slow Air* (Picador, 2002)

Neil Rollinson – *A Spillage of Mercury* (Cape Poetry, 1996)

Anne Rouse – *Timing* (Bloodaxe Books, 1997)

Jacob Sam-La Rose – *Breaking Silence* (Bloodaxe Books, 2011)

Noo Saro-Wiwa – *Looking for Transwonderland: Travels in Nigeria*
(Granta Publications, 2013)

Jo Shapcott – *Electroplating the Baby* (Bloodaxe, 1988)

Ruth Sharman – *Birth of the Owl Butterflies* (Picador, 1997)

Ken Smith – *Wild Root* (Bloodaxe, 1998)

Ken Smith – *Wormwood* (Bloodaxe, 1987)

Martin Stokes – *The First Death of Venice* (Bloodaxe Books, 1987)

Matthew Sweeney – *A Smell of Fish* (Cape Poetry, 2000)

George Szirtes – *The Budapest File* (Bloodaxe Books, 2000)

Charles Tomlinson – *The Return* (Oxford Poets, 1987)

Jack Underwood – *Happiness* (Faber and Faber, 2015)

Luke Wright – *What I Learned from Johnny Bevan*
(Penned in the Margins, 2016)

Malcolm X – *The Autobiography of Malcolm X* (Penguin Books, 2007)

Dance the Guns to Silence: 100 Poems for Ken Saro-Wiwa Edited by Nii
Ayikwei Parkes and Kadija Sesay (Flipped Eye Publishing, 2005)

The Best of Poetry London, 1988 - 2013 – Edited by Tim Dooley and
Martha Kapos (Carcanet Press, 2014)

Acknowledgements

We gratefully acknowledge the following publishers, poets, and rights holders who have given permission for their poems to be reproduced and included in this publication as follows:

Iain Crichton Smith: 'No Return' from *The Exiles* (Carcanet Press Limited, 1984).

Carol Ann Duffy: 'Letters From Deadmen' from *Collected Poems* by Carol Ann Duffy. Published by Picador, 2015. Copyright © Carol Ann Duffy. Reproduced by permission of the author c/o Rogers, Coleridge & White Ltd., 20 Powis Mews, London W111JN

Michael Hofmann: 'Albion Market' from *Acrimony* (Faber and Faber Limited, 1986).

Seamus Heaney: 'A Shooting Script' from *The Haw Lantern* (Faber and Faber Limited, 1987).

Jo Shapcott: 'Photograph: Sheepshearing (Northlew, 1917)' from *Electroplating the Baby* (Bloodaxe, 1988).

Charles Boyle: 'Writ in Water' from *The Best of Poetry London 1989 (Poetry and Prose, 1988 – 2013)*, (Carcanet 1989).

Robert Crawford: 'Transformer' from *A Scottish Assembly* (Chatto & Windus, 1990), ISBN 07011 3595 6. Permission kindly granted by Random House.

Sarah Maguire: 'Still At Sea' from *Spilt Milk* (Secker and Warburg, 1991), ISBN 0-436-27095-1. Copyright © Sarah Maguire. Permission kindly granted by the poet.

Simon Armitage: 'Not the Furniture Game', from *Kid* (Faber and Faber Limited, 1992 / 2002).

Moniza Alvi: 'Map of India', from *Split World: Poems 1990-2005* (Bloodaxe Books, 2008) www.bloodaxebooks.com

W.N. Herbert: 'The King and Queen of Dumfriesshire', from *Cabaret McGonagall* (Bloodaxe Books, 1996), 1-85224-353-8

Elizabeth Bartlett: 'Life Sentence', from *Appetites of Love* (Bloodaxe Books, 2001) ISBN 1-85224-548-4 www.bloodaxebooks.com

Neil Rollinson: 'The Ecstasy of St Saviour's Avenue', from *A Spillage of Mercury* (Cape Poetry, 1996), ISBN 0-224-04008-1. Permission kindly granted by the poet.

Ruth Sharman: 'Fury', from *Birth of the Owl Butterflies* (Picador, 1997). Permission kindly granted by the poet.

Ken Smith: 'Before the Lisbon tribunal', from *Shed: Poems 1980-2001* (Bloodaxe Books, 2002) www.bloodaxebooks.com

Frieda Hughes: 'Fire 1', p. 40, from *Wooroloo* (Bloodaxe Books, 1999), ISBN 1-85224-496-8 www.bloodaxebooks.com

Douglas Dunn: 'A European Dream' from *The Year's Afternoon* (Faber and Faber Limited, 2000).

Pascale Petit: 'My Father's Lungs' from *The Zoo Father* (Seren, 2001).

Andrew Motion: From 'A Long Story - 3. The Aftermath' from *Public Property* (2001 Faber and Faber Limited).